The Joy of Wintering

The Joy of Wintering

of

How to Rest, Reconnect
and Rejuvenate with
Creativity and Conscious Living

Erin Niimi Longhurst

HarperCollins*Publishers*

HarperCollins*Publishers*
1 London Bridge Street
London SE1 9GF

www.harpercollins.co.uk

HarperCollins*Publishers*
Macken House, 39/40 Mayor Street Upper
Dublin 1, D01 C9W8, Ireland

First published by HarperCollins*Publishers* 2024

13 5 7 9 10 8 6 4 2

A catalogue record of this book is available from the British Library

ISBN 978-0-00-865330-9

Printed and bound by PNB, Latvia

While the author of this work has made every effort to ensure that the information
contained in this book is as accurate and up-to-date as possible at the time of publication,
medical and pharmaceutical knowledge is constantly changing and the application of it
to particular circumstances depends on many factors. Therefore it is recommended that
readers always consult a qualified medical specialist for individual advice. This book
should not be used as an alternative to seeking specialist medical advice which should be
sought before any action is taken. The author and publishers cannot be held responsible for
any errors and omissions that may be found in the text, or any actions that may be taken by
a reader as a result of any reliance on the information contained in the text which is taken
entirely at the reader's own risk.

This book contains FSC™ certified paper and other controlled sources to ensure
responsible forest management.

For more information visit: www.harpercollins.co.uk/green

Contents

Introduction
Wintering for a creative life

*If Winter comes,
can Spring be
far behind?*

—Percy Bysshe Shelley

Why Wintering Matters

The year is 2018. I am 26 years old, and although I don't know it yet, I'm about to receive a wake-up call. It takes the form of a state-issued alert, warning residents and visitors to the beautiful state of Hawaii that a ballistic missile is inbound, and imminent. This news has the effect of making me feel both weightless and anchored at the same time – unable to move, while my thoughts and emotions speed away from me. Despite being moments from death (if this message is anything to go by), my mother and I spend what little time we have left together, as usual, bickering. She accuses me of being dramatic, before suggesting I take cover in her apartment building's pungent garbage room, where I can seek shelter from the threat of shattering glass – a fear I didn't know I had until I started screaming at her to keep away from the windows. In the face of her nonchalance, I angrily accuse her of never taking anything seriously, before suggesting that we lie down holding hands, as images of Pompeii spring to my mind, prompted by the view of the volcanic landscape from her living room window and the sight of the extinct tuff cone of Koko Crater.

We do none of these things. Instead, I send a series of embarrassing messages to friends – pledging my undying love and affection for them. I text poorly behaved ex-boyfriends assurances of my forgiveness and continued friendship, which I find myself wanting to retract at a later date. Years later, my mother and I would laugh about the events of that morning. To this day, she still holds a grudge about the fact that I refused to let her go run her originally scheduled errand for that day (getting her car seen to), while I have to remind her that our neighbours threw their children down manholes in an attempt to find safety.

We needn't have worried; it was all for naught – a false alert after all that left many of us feeling like the naked emperor in the old folktale. At least we could take comfort in the fact that we weren't alone in our foolishness.

It was a week after that incident, on my flight back to London, when I first felt that something had shifted within me. It was as though I had become attuned to the perfect frequency, open to the limitless possibilities of my life that had been previously obscured. Everything had a sweetness and musicality to it not present before, and I had a sense of unadulterated joy at the prospect of creating things. Like I had been created for that purpose; the feeling swept me up in its ebb and flow, and I found myself gorging on it all.

The next few months after the incident resulted in a sudden burst of activity, a series of events that would've felt like a lucky streak had I not been putting them into motion myself. My first book was published the following April. I spent the year travelling, finding myself clients in places I'd always wanted to explore and then spending meaningful time there. I made the decision to move back to New York. These impulsive and rapid-fire decisions that I was making made me feel light-headed and giddy, and I felt free, and present, and alive – as if my metaphorical brush with death had given me a free pass to be the most audacious version of myself. I felt untouchable and invincible, young and beautiful – completely naive and utterly thoughtless. I moved, driven by impulse. While I had the vague sense that I was trying to shake something off, or elude something, I dismissed the thought peevishly. I threw myself a leaving do, taking over several tables at the back of a pub, lined with all the houseplants I couldn't take with me, and all the electrical products I didn't manage to sell. 'Leaving a trail of broken hearts behind you!' read one note on my leaving card. If only I had known that one of them was my own.

The New York I moved back to, unsurprisingly, was not the New York of my childhood. As a result it felt like diving into a pool, only to have misjudged the temperature – both familiar and unfamiliar, bitter and sweet at the same time. Some things hadn't changed – the doorman at my dad's old apartment building still recognized me from when I was a kid – but I felt out of sync with the pace of the city. This was compounded by the financial hit that accompanies a transatlantic move – I had given myself a couple of months to save after I'd furnished my matchbox of a studio apartment, before promising myself that after that I could properly enjoy New York at its best. Once I had the chance to regroup, *then* I could eat well, drink in the sights, see all the latest exhibitions and shows and regain that sense of *ikigai* – or purpose – that I had before.

In the meantime, despite my pledge to shed my entire London self, I had already found myself unable and unwilling to do so. Nine days after I had made my big move, a boy from Oxford whose number I had saved on my phone as 'not serious summer fling' booked himself onto a flight out to see me. I buy him a Reuben from Katz's Delicatessen and take him to a baseball game, and after a day of drinking pina coladas on Coney Island he decides to take a year out of his medical training to move out here with me. I feel effervescent with all the possibilities and incandescently happy. By this point, it's September 2019, so all he has to do is tie up a few loose ends and by March the next year, it'll be a done deal. What could go wrong?

A 'rough couple of years' is such a quintessentially British descriptor – alluding to a period of pain, confusion and fear while

simultaneously dismissing and trivializing the time spent, minimizing it somehow. The stiff upper lip, and so on. It has been a *rough couple of years* since my time in New York. The year 2020, for example, became the year that crying on video calls became standard practice – or at least it did for me. I cried when a childhood friend lost a sibling but had to mourn alone because they were at risk. I cried as I spent fifty-five days without being in the same room as another person. I cried as my casual summer boyfriend and his other medic colleagues heroically tried to stem the flow caused by a devastating virus spoken about at first in rumoured whispers. I cried as they put their lives on the line, working through the confusion and the sheer incompetence of their leaders, only to have it all be thrown in their faces later. I moved back to the UK to support him. During that time, I saw in myself and others the ways in which fear and stress become pain. The state of constant upheaval meant I was – and still am – very much adrift. Despite it all, I'm very much one of the lucky ones.

I find myself staring at a photo – of me, tanned, in an orange bikini, clutching a jug of margarita – while sat in the slick chairs of my local A&E walk-in centre. Three years have passed since that day drinking cocktails on the waterfront, and I'm now in England. It's the fourth time this year that I'm back in the hospital, doubled over with an abdominal pain that is becoming increasingly frequent. On a good day, the presence of the pain feels like an unwelcome pest at a picnic – lazily swatted away, but not detracting from the festivities. But today is a bad day, and the aching in my abdomen has grown so much that I'd been prostrate on the floor of the bathroom at work for half an hour, before conceding defeat and coming to hospital. Those that say 'mind over matter' have clearly never had any unexplained recurring health issues.

*Wisdom comes
with winters.*

—Oscar Wilde

I ended up in A&E six times in total, before I finally found someone who heard me. She sat with me while I cried – tears of relief, this time – and helped me find ways to manage and stay on top of the chronic pain that still feels latent. Those years of uncertainty, however, robbed me of the ways in which I used to find my sense of self, the ways in which I would tap the well of my creativity. I felt a sense of despair, as if my life had been razed. I'd burned it to the ground by tempting fate with my youthful arrogance. The audaciousness of my past had caught up with me, and this was my punishment. What followed was a time of stillness, discovery and reflection.

❄ ❄ ❄

Before I was born, my Grandfather Peter kept bees. By the time I was old enough to scrape my knees gorging myself on plums from his orchard, all that was left of his beekeeping days were tales enshrined in our family lore. Stories of him embarrassing my aunts by donning his beekeeping outfit at their birthday parties always make the rounds, but I was forever fascinated by the ghosts of his apiary past – the old wooden beehives which lay vacant, their white paint flaking off in the winter snow. I wanted to know what we could learn from the small but mighty honeybee.

THE WINTER OF THE HONEYBEE

Unlike bumblebees or other varieties of solitary bees, honeybee colonies survive the bleak winters by remaining active in their hives, clustering together for warmth and drawing upon their stores for survival. While the worker bees of the summer, who industriously work away at their role of collecting pollen and nectar, have a lifespan of around six weeks, the honeybees of winter, responsible for getting the colony through the bitter cold, live for up to five months.

A HONEYBEE'S YEAR

Winter: The winter bees, in survival mode, focus their energy on generating heat and protecting the Queen until late winter, when she begins to lay the worker bees in time for spring.

Spring: The first worker bees will go to meet the blooming flowers and begin to raise the new drones as the population swells.

Summer: The short-lived worker bees collect nectar and pollen, working away to make honey and add to their stores – the hive is at its fullest at this time.

Autumn: The Queen will begin to lay the eggs that will become the 'winter bees', hardier than their summertime counterparts due to the difference in their physiology, enabling them to withstand the brutal conditions of winter. The drones are expelled.

*Let us love winter,
for it is the spring
of genius.*

—Pietro Aretino

My abrupt departure from New York felt soul-wrenching. I had burned myself out creatively and professionally and suddenly every decision appeared to be teeming with guilt, a cocktail of shame and fear. As life around me seemingly resumed, the stakes suddenly felt higher, and yet I remained in a state of arrested development. I'd share some carefully crafted prose online, but a mindlessly produced and often catty meme would outperform it massively on social media, so I stopped posting altogether. The online community was not giving me any answers – and certainly no joy – but I wasn't sure exactly where else to look.

Wanting a solution, and afraid I'd become too complacent, I left a company I had worked at for close to a decade. I decided to take a leap of faith and began a new job at a local restaurant, keen to help it grow, as I had done at my previous role, by doing a bit of everything – working in the kitchens, managing their communications – while using the time to fulfil my dream of opening my own restaurant one day, by learning on the job. But very quickly the new venture soured; the owners had no firm business plan, pivoting from seasonal small

plates and fresh pasta to takeaway pizzas within the first few months. This scattergun approach, combined with an industry still recovering from the previous year of uncertainty, meant that the restaurant soon folded, and with it my sense of confidence and self-worth.

What kept me afloat during that time was the sanctuary provided by my grandmother's home, her garden and her calming presence. A widow since my grandfather's passing in 2015, my grandmother continues to lovingly tend to her garden, which in turn supplies her with an abundance of roses, seasonal flowers, fruits, herbs and all manner of vegetables for her efforts. Her garden room is full of bottled fruit and homemade chutneys and jams, which through its contents reveals a sense of a family history, marking the passage of time and the changing of the seasons, year after year. To me, she demonstrates the finest example of kindness and strength – her diligence and determination producing sustenance and beauty. The garden is a project she began with my grandfather, but one that has not only endured loss and grief but serves as a living example of endurance – life after loss, exquisite in its persisting.

We are more of the earth than we are of machine. A fact that never ceases to make me laugh is that we have genetically more in common with a banana than, say, a mobile phone. Yet we are increasingly at the mercy of unfeeling algorithmic updates – ever more detached from the natural world around us, which is in a constant state of flux and danger due to our own hand. The answers we seek can often be found through the examples around us – but we just need to be paying attention.

The land we tend allows us to feast, but also requires time to be fallow – not to lie dormant or idle, but to recoup. Replenish, conserve and build reserves. The tumultuous journey of the last few years has

INTRODUCTION

shown me this, in spades. Take mine as a cautionary tale – I did not take the time to rest, and so I was forced to. What I discovered, and what helped me, were the ways in which I could connect with myself. To rekindle a sense of affection and kindness, but also to reset my creativity. To cleanse my palate and to feel rejuvenation and satiety in my work, rather than the taste of bitter disappointment. I did this through asking help of friends and loved ones, and not going through it in isolation. The first time I felt like myself in a long time was when I had reached out to a friend wanting companionship, and caught them using my old, trusted coffee grinder – the one I had given them stewardship over during my sojourn to New York – to grate Parmesan cheese. I was warmed by the invitation to dinner through laughter (and only a little bit of mock horror) I reconnected with my former self (and rescued my abused grinder from a terrible fate).

The metaphor of the life cycle of a honeybee colony, and the way it adapts and evolves to endure and thrive as the seasons change, is one I draw upon in this book when approaching my own creative process. From the bees' approach to wintering to their forward-thinking behaviour during the abundant months of summer, I traced a similar trajectory in the ways in which I began to adapt when crafting a more thoughtful practice for my own productions – whether it was through my writing or any other artistic endeavour I set my mind to.

A grounding technique commonly used by those experiencing physical and mental distress is one that encourages the use of our senses – to identify things that we can see, hear, touch, smell and taste – until we reach a state of relative calm. In The Things We See, I focus on the ways in which inspiration can strike us, how we can absorb and find beauty in our environment to spark creativity. I examine What to Listen Out For in the next chapter, embracing silence and stillness as we work through these ideas; these two chapters represent the poignant dormancy of the winter period.

Through What We Touch and How We Breathe, we move into the tentative exploration of spring and the confidence of summer before we begin to wind down and move on once we've shared – but not without first savouring flavour through How to Taste.

As the honeybee colony evolves and changes with each passing year and season, so do our pursuits, and through this work I hope to demonstrate the ways in which the moments of stillness – the quieter times in our life – when, perhaps, we are in survival mode of one kind or another, are all part of a greater good, a higher purpose. To not confuse these times as being wasted, or unimportant, but to recognize the role they play in allowing us to flourish and thrive, to grow and succeed.

HOW WE CAN SUPPORT BEES IN WINTER

Whether it's the industrious honeybee or any other bee that might be waking from hibernation, these are some of the ways in which we can support them over the winter period.

✳ **Avoid digging and leave dead stems undisturbed.**
   Hibernating bees like bumblebees will be
   waiting winter out underground, so try
   to avoid disturbing their habitat and
   this vital period of slumber.

   ✳ **Plant early-blooming flowers.** Crocuses
      and other early flowering plants provide
      sustenance for bees in the months where
      this might be harder to come by.

✳ **Make sugar syrup.** If you see a solitary winter
   bee that seems to be struggling – which can
   sometimes happen on the rare, warm winter's
   day – and there are no flowering plants nearby,
   you can help it replenish its stores by providing
   a sugar syrup solution. A small amount of sugar
   syrup (with a 2:1 sugar to water ratio) can provide
   energy and temporary sustenance until the bee can
   gather strength.

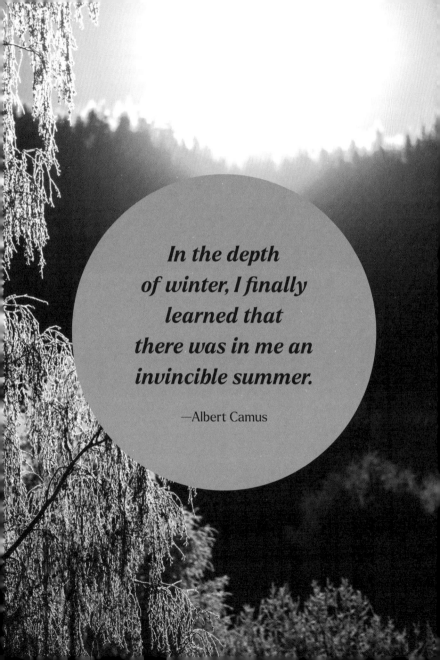

In the depth of winter, I finally learned that there was in me an invincible summer.

—Albert Camus

We live during a time of forced abundance – constantly on the go, everything happening rapid fire – yet we often feel like we are missing out. We want what we don't have. We crave more and work harder to earn it. We sleep less, do more, go faster. It feels like we are flowers forced to bloom too soon – before conditions are optimal. We wither and fade, frustrated, tired, put out. With this book, I want to prioritize rest. Welcome slower living, to spark curiosity, feel centred and instil hope through wintering. Like the hive of bees in winter, humming away and saving their strength, I want us to encourage ourselves and others to embrace the cyclical nature of life. To better understand the ebbs and flows, and recognize patterns in ourselves in order to become more resilient. Not only to seek beauty in our moments of sadness and downtime but to find inspiration through them. This is how I worked through periods of creative block and emotional turmoil – and while what worked for me might not work for everyone, it might help you to recognize the tools and methods of self-soothing that will resonate with you or others close to you. To understand that, as part of nature ourselves, we also need to find the time to embrace dormancy, drawing in part from global traditions and cultures that have honed ways to build resilience through seeking comfort, rest and warmth (both physically and emotionally).

I've written this book to support those who feel stuck and trapped, as I have done – both in their emotional and creative relationships with themselves and with others. Perhaps you've had a setback and are seeking to find a sense of clarity, to better equip yourself with the tools you need to weather the uncertain, tumultuous times. This is a book for those who want to find ways in which they can not only begin a creative project but complete it – and continue to do so, over and over again. But it is also for those who want to be

able to create, without wearing themselves into the ground – to find a cyclical pattern that works for them, to tie into the ebb and flow of their life – however that might be.

The goal of this pursuit, ultimately, is joy. The thread running through my works to date has focused on contentment and the importance of compassion, but after a series of setbacks I shifted my focus elsewhere. I was falling into disruptive patterns, seeking

INTRODUCTION

validation in all the wrong places – losing touch with myself by seeking to find meaning in the superficial. Much like artificial sweetener, it purported to serve the same function, but it just didn't taste the same (and most definitely wasn't going to be good for me in the long run).

Joy is simple. It doesn't have to cost anything. Infant children and family pets demonstrate their understanding of this form of pleasure without using language at all. They find amusement and wonder in things and demonstrate this as a source of happiness to the loved ones around them. It can be infectious – there are those from whom it seems to flow in abundance, and those people often have an almost magnetic quality to them. The simplicity of joy – or exhilarating delight – can lead us to believe that it is *easy*. For some of us, however, this is not always so. Sometimes the flame burns bright and sometimes we need a bit more kindling. We need to find ways to create more sparks to help the fire get going. To work to attain our prize. To prepare for those times when it might not come.

What follows are the actions, tips, mindsets, mental images, quotes and advice I've found myself turning to over time. The things I've found helpful, and which have informed the way I've framed this book, and the insights I've gathered along the way. During the course of writing it I've been shaken by an emotional betrayal, gone through a period of financial instability and navigated a bout of ill health. While I have sometimes felt like an imposter writing a book of this kind, I hope that the wisdom, kindness and hope I've received from others and from myself has somehow distilled itself in these pages. That together, we can build strength through wintering. To fight through the inhospitable cold and find inner strength, allowing us to bloom and create sweetness, come spring.

Chapter 1

The Things We See
How we can receive inspiration

If you cry because the sun
has gone out of your life,
your tears will prevent you
from seeing the stars.

—Icelandic Proverb

In order to live a fulfilled and creative life, I believe we must cultivate a sense of curiosity, and carve out the space in our life to do so. It's of no surprise to me that the kindest and happiest people I know are those who understand that the secret to finding joy is to relentlessly pursue a sense of wonder. To dedicate their lives – at least in part – to creating and seeking beauty, whether it's through honing a craft, taking the time to appreciate a new exhibition, or even just to notice the way the moon waxes and wanes. Those with the power to see beyond – not in the supernatural sense, but to engage with the world around them with hope – remain open to all the possibilities that the world offers. We often regard those who see the world through rose-tinted glasses with disparagement, but things can go too far the other way; people remain stuck and discontented when they don't have a dedicated gratitude practice or are lumbered with an outlook clouded by cynicism.

My move back from New York coincided with a period of career upheaval. The enforced period of isolation, therefore, compounded the feelings I had of uncertainty and fear. Desperate for a human connection, I spent more time than ever scrolling through various social media platforms, seeking to replicate that feeling of trust, desperate to feel understood, and seen. As I was shown more products I didn't need or couldn't afford, repeatedly presented with a sanitized and inauthentic version of reality, I fell deeper into a state of loneliness, full of self-loathing and pity. Yet I was also aware of how grateful I should be and how lucky I was – so this disconnect compounded my emotions.

It's incredibly telling that Silicon Valley executives rarely let their young children near devices of any kind. To me, this is revealing of how insidious and harmful it all is – those algorithms are designed to be addictive. Companies become profitable by selling you things you don't need, and make you feel terrible in the process to keep you engaged. On one level I instinctively understood this, and yet I had built a career on digital storytelling. I was part of the problem, in a hostage situation of my own making. It has become an almost essential part of modern life. Short of renouncing society altogether, it is incredibly difficult to detach yourself from these communication platforms and tools without risking alienating yourself further. How do we strike the balance?

For me, the choice comes from making a conscious decision to be an active participant. My own creative process can come only from taking inspiration from my direct surroundings and being attuned to my immediate environment. The technology we have available

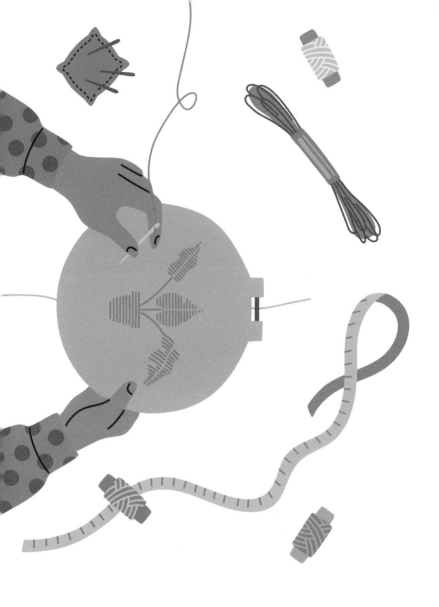

THE THINGS WE SEE

to us currently provides us access to every single language in the world, every type of ballpoint pen that has ever been in existence or thousands of ways to cook with rhubarb – and yet how often do we seek things out for ourselves, rather than have them served to us? Information delivered to us in this way, without us having sought it out ourselves, often feels like it lacks satiety. In my most unproductive and unfulfilled periods, I would find myself frittering away countless hours, exhausting myself, and yet feeling wholly unsatisfied. I'd overwhelm myself with information, and content, and yet feel listless, like I was missing something. Like I was looking for something else instead, only I didn't quite know what – I was suppressing my own thirst for curiosity. I was looking for wonder and enchantment in all the wrong places, and with it grew my discontent.

The transformation of my creative process came from becoming more selective with the things I seek out, by which I mean the types of content I consume. For this I've developed a hard-and-fast rule: if I haven't actively sought it, I don't invest any meaningful time into it – or when I do, I have guidelines I adhere to about it.

1. **Have I actively sought this information out?** Being 'chronically online' is a phrase that is often seen as a badge of honour, but I firmly believe that there is only so much we can process at any one time. We are expected to be constantly reachable, never taking our fingers off the pulse – a fact exacerbated by the sheer volume of information we are presented with from everywhere, all of the time. It is relentless and overwhelming, and a fact that contributed to my sense of burnout. These days, I try to set time limits on when I engage with different forms of media, for example getting my news from the radio in the morning or when I'm on a lunch break, rather than responding to a constant stream of notifications served to me. Rather than having this 'pushed' upon me, I choose when to 'pull' the information I need, at a time I control.

2. **Will this deepen my relationships?** Rather than seek validation from an audience I don't know, I try to prioritize and deepen connections and relationships I have in real life. If my fellow Sunday morning dog walkers mention an account that might be of interest to me, I'm more likely to take them up on the recommendation; maybe a friend who lives far away from me has reached out because they want someone to discuss a new series with so I'll check it out.

3. **How much time am I willing to spend on this, and are there more meaningful ways to do so?** Could this time be better spent getting to know myself? To know others?

This journey to better understanding the ways in which I could harness my sense of creativity has come from truly acknowledging just how much of myself I was willing to give up. My investment – of time and energy – into being mindlessly served to, rather than being an active and curious participant, often came at the cost of losing a sense of self, rather than gaining anything from it. If people had an opinion on my work, or thought that others were doing it better, or living more authentically, then who was I to say any different? Surrounded by these intrusive thoughts and an abundance of perspectives showing only what I lacked, I became further untethered from my own passions. I wasn't being served anything of substance, but it was because I had forgotten the secret all along – that the journey is as important as the destination. Magic, wonder and satisfaction come from connecting the dots yourself. That's what ignites the spark – and it will be unique for you and your story.

The serendipitous discoveries are the stuff that dreams are made of.

Changing the ways we see

The most poignant lesson I've ever learned about being open and receptive to your sense of fun – which is ruled by your inner child, the guardian of your creativity – came from a person I've never met, whose name I will probably never know but who provided me a sense of whimsy and entertainment during a time when it was dearly needed.

My studio apartment in the East Village of New York City overlooked the backyards of the other tenement-style houses that lined my block. These identical shoebox flats, all with wrought-iron fire escapes, looked out onto these backyards, but the neighbourhood became eerily quiet during the first lockdown. Usually filled with NYU and Columbia students, who decided to make their way home to weather out this period of uncertainty, the neighbourhood became so quiet that at one point the loudest sounds to wake me up in the morning were birdsong. Only a few of us in those apartment buildings remained, and the usually vibrant and bustling neighbourhood seemed like a pale and anaemic version of its former self. My sister, the only relative of mine who lived nearby, was heavily pregnant, and the uncertain nature of everything during that time led us to take precautions – even a casual catch-up over a cup of tea was out of bounds – so despite how close we were geographically, in a tense and fearful climate our usual routines seemed too much of a risk. I was, like many others during that time, completely devoid of any human company.

Seemingly overnight, the outside world had become uninviting and scary, and I was overcome by a sense of desolation and despair. The days were stifling, with a vice-like grip of monotony and repetition. The hours blended together, and despite my best efforts to keep my wits about me, I was often not even sure what day it was because I'd lost track so long ago. That is, until I became aware of some animated activity visible from the home of my neighbours. Over the course of just one week, they had thrown themselves a Hawaiian-themed luau party, only to decorate for Halloween a day later, before erecting and dressing a Christmas tree – all during a week in mid-April. It was nonsensical, totally ridiculous and utterly silly – and yet, full of joy.

What their rationale and reasoning was is something I thought of often, and something I'm sure I will never know. The absurdity and frivolousness of it opened my eyes to the possibility of finding happiness and whimsy during even the most mundane and yet trying of times. That real contentment and fulfilment comes at the expense of looking a bit ridiculous – yet even in the most confined spaces, it is possible to evoke the majesty of all the seasons in a day.

Finding Creative Inspiration

Inspiration can come from anywhere – we just have to be open to receiving it. As a writer, I find myself being somewhat magpie-like in my approach, saving memories and feelings to draw upon later. Over the time I was unwell, or during any period where I struggle with feeling blocked or uninspired, I find that this ability becomes suppressed. It can feel all-encompassing, and it is hard to see the wood for the trees.

When you struggle to find inspiration, it can feel like you are adrift at sea with a broken compass. You lose direction, and the path forward is hard to navigate. In my case, I felt stagnant and stationary – unable to make any decisions because I felt so overwhelmed. With that feeling came a sense of shame. Shame loves stagnation – it becomes a fertile ground to multiply and grow. Worrying that it was contagious, I would close myself off and isolate from others.

The productivity trap can be partially blamed for this. We prioritize rest and play when we raise children, but do not afford the same courtesy to ourselves. Framing these 'winter' periods not to bring forth and produce, but as part of a dedicated time of introspection and reflection, is vital. Some of the more compelling insights I gained during the times when I simply did not have the

THE THINGS WE SEE

capacity to create anything of value. I began to notice that the times when my energy – both physical and emotional – was depleted, heightened my sense of perception. It kept me open to receiving new perspective and noticing subtleties and nuances I may have overlooked without it.

Find distinctions in times for play and for rest. Do so greedily, and with gusto – without shame, or guilt. Read more. Seek more beauty. Focus on finer details and look at the bigger picture. Find new plants, follow new paths and look for new patterns, without the pressure of doing so to create or complete anything. Cancel plans. Then, you can take a blank canvas and fill it with colour, light and texture. Others might share your perspective, but no one can replicate your eye, or see the things you do. When seeking a new creative project or bringing something new to the world, first you must understand the world around you – drinking it all in, filing it away for later.

Planting the Seed

I've never met a gardener I didn't get on with. Which is to say, I hold a deep affection for those who diligently work to achieve their vision, who can appreciate the magnitude and wonder of seeing something (given the right conditions) flourish and bear fruit. I play the happy role of project manager (by heavily delegating) when it comes to my own garden, but I cannot deny the sense of immense pride and satisfaction that comes with cutting flowers you've grown from seed or picking cherry tomatoes from your very own vine. We are custodians of the earth, and there is something awe-inspiring and humbling about what we are able to accomplish with it – it just requires us to prepare the ground and tend to the land.

How does your creative garden grow?

One of the things that comes from spending time in your own garden is suddenly realizing that you are able to identify which of the seeds you planted are annuals, biennials or perennials – something that you learn the hard way, after waiting patiently for several years for the lovely pink flowers that you were so fond of to bloom and spring up again, only to realize that it doesn't quite work that way.

The same thing goes for activities, projects and endeavours. For a very long time, I would count lack of longevity as a mark of failure, and it was only when accepting that not every pursuit or path I take needs to be part of a long career that I could appreciate them at face value. Some things you only try once, for a short time – but you can find satisfaction and growth in that, too.

Annual plants only live for one growing season: germinating, blooming, setting seed and dying within the space of a year. Biennials take a little longer to get going – you might germinate the seed one year and benefit from the results the following year. Perennials in contrast last longer, with the potential to flower for several years. I like having projects and hobbies that I can pick up and pursue in varying degrees of focus and dedication – practices that I might dedicate years to, in contrast to classes I might try on a whim. It allows me to have one foot out of my comfort zone, without putting all my eggs in one basket, and so alleviating that fear of failure. In times when I feel an abundance of pressure, this approach helps me to find moments of joy and levity. Rather than thinking of it as being scatty, I like to think of it as giving my creative garden a bit of texture; this organic approach to ways of living is actually healthier and allows us to be more resilient to times of change because of it – just as in a garden.

Plants that grow without soil

Back when I was living in a studio apartment, I developed a mild obsession with plants that could grow without soil. Whether it was an aversion to having to lug bags of compost up a third-floor walk-up I don't know, but I suspect it had something to do with being able to see the process unfolding in front of me – like the secrets of the universe. Seeing so visibly the development of growth was a humbling and awe-inspiring lesson. Here are some of my favourites:

Tillandsia: Also known as the air plant, this hardy plant hails from Mexico and South America. Their wiry, sage green appearance always brightens up a space; these are perhaps the hardiest houseplants for even the most neglectful of plant parents.

Lucky Bamboo: Preferring warm and humid temperatures, the *Dracaena sanderiana* is a symbol of prosperity and fortune in many cultures. This has been attributed to the rapid speed at which it propagates, and is incorporated into homes as an auspicious plant, symbolizing wealth and prosperity according to the principles of feng shui.

Orchids: As orchids mature, certain varieties are able to survive without soil as long as their roots receive enough moisture to ensure their survival.

Amaryllis: These favour tight pots – I've had to chide my partner several times as he's mistakenly killed off mine by lovingly repotting them into a roomier home. These have a special place in my heart as several years ago my aunt gave me and my cousins a plant each for Christmas. Living in different parts of the country, our various plants flower at different times of the year, and we have a chat dedicated to sharing when they do so. Spending much of the year resembling an onion, the amaryllis often shoots up and blooms in the most dramatic and beautiful way. What started out as a family tradition has now become a winter gift I give to a few close friends during the festive season (particularly when I'm stuck for inspiration during a time of almost constant gift-giving). I adore the amaryllis-related updates as a way of checking in, and as a prompt for staying in touch, mirroring the ways we each bloom and grow, too. A metaphor, in some ways, of the gentle care friendships require too.

Philodendron: The heart-shaped leaves of the philodendron are perfect for propagating – almost like giving away bits of your heart to friends and family to take with them.

TAKE CARE OF HOUSEPLANTS IN WINTER (AND THEY WILL TAKE CARE OF YOU)

* **Avoid temperature extremes** – not too hot, not too cold. Keep away from any cold draughts and the heat of fires (or your radiator).

* **Remember not to fertilize** or feed your plant this time of year – less is more during this period of rest.

* **Water less frequently** than you would during warmer months.

In addition to purifying the air, houseplants have the ability to help soothe our minds, and bring a sense of contentment and happiness to our surroundings.[1] [2] Perhaps this is because it allows us to feel closer to the natural world – to consciously remind ourselves that we are part of something greater.

*One's shadow
grows larger than life
when admired by the
light of the moon.*

—Chinese Proverb

The Phases of the Moon

Throughout my childhood and adolescence, my mother would always predict the outbreak of familial discord in our household by blaming it on the potency of the full moon. While it has taken me a very long time to come around to the idea, I've begun to actively seek knowing which phase of the lunar cycle we are currently in, if only to satisfy my own curiosity. Unlike the bright magnetism of the sun, the moon serves as a metaphor for the fluctuations in our energy – our intuition, and the multiple shades of emotion, action and feeling we experience each day.

As someone who experiences menstruation, the 28-day cycle also serves as a useful tool for checking in with my energy levels, particularly when it comes to setting intentions or describing where I am physically when making plans with friends.

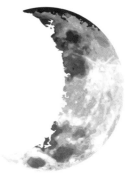

New Moon: The sun and moon are on the same side of the earth. A time for new beginnings and past reflections, where we might need to gather strength to prepare for the journey ahead.

Waxing Crescent Moon: The sun moves closer to the moon and begins to illuminate the crescent. It is a time to move towards actions, to set intentions and move forward with hope.

First Quarter Moon: Now is the time to proceed, with caution – exactly half of the moon is illuminated, and the intentions and hopes we have set in the first quarter begin to be put into action.

Waxing Gibbous Moon: Steer the course – most of the moon is illuminated, and you should continue to build and grow towards the goals you have set, mindfully maintaining your focus.

Full Moon: The sun is completely illuminating the moon, and it is at this stage that you should reap the benefits – the intentions you have set so far are in fruition, and what has previously been obscured should become visibly apparent.

Waning Gibbous Moon: As the moon begins to wane, this calls for a period of gratitude and considered, thoughtful reflection – moving forward with serenity and grace.

Third Quarter Moon: If the first quarter moon invited you to proceed with hope and caution, now is the time to let go of things that no longer serve you.

Waning Crescent Moon: Now is the time for reflection and rest before the cycle turns towards a new beginning.

Tracking your cycle and how to do it

In the last fifteen years, the most transformative thing I have done where it comes to my mental and physical health has been tracking how different factors are affected by my menstrual cycle. Before then, my bursts of creativity and energy, or sluggish approach to mornings and periods of negative self-talk, seemed as though random and disconnected. Until I began to take the time to notice and record the changes in my body and mental state, or the patterns began to reveal themselves to me, I lacked cohesion – which made me unreliable, at the whim of forces larger than me that I failed to understand.

It can be as simple as noting down the state of your skin – whether it's blemished more than usual, or positively glowing. The ways in which your sense of smell is heightened, or how frequently you find yourself snapping, unprovoked, at those around you. The act of putting it *down* helps you to keep on top – and I now try to plan the ways in which I approach projects so that they coincide, where possible, with where I might be in my cycle. During certain phases I feel more solitary, and this is when I get my ideas down, or focus on the editing. Or during times when my skin feels clear and I find myself effervescent and full of energy, I take a more collaborative approach – sharing my work more widely or soliciting feedback.

I oscillate between using various apps, or just good old pen and paper on my calendar, but the best way to track is by making it a habit – a daily one, but not one too arduous that it becomes a task you markedly avoid. For myself, I like to note down:

* Confidence levels (how am I feeling that day, on a scale of one to five?)
* Energy levels
* What is my focus on today?
* Do I feel any discomfort?
* What is my skin like today?
* Do I have any cravings?
* How have my personal interactions been today?

At the end of each month, look at what you have noted to see any patterns. I like to do this quarterly and annually too, in order to get a bigger picture – to truly understand the ways in which my mood can fluctuate, and so I can continue – where possible – to proactively protect those spaces of rest and relaxation within my schedule. Particularly when you are working towards achieving or creating something, sustaining the momentum can be a greater challenge than the act of creating itself; finding these patterns and being able to not only prepare but harness these waves of energy can feel transformative.

The Beauty of the Mundane, Yet Remarkable

There is something comforting and melodic about the patterns revealed to us by nature. The fact that every single snowflake is unique is awe-inspiring to contemplate when you admire the snow-capped mountains in the depths of winter. Seeking ways to capture the ever-changing, ephemeral nature of the world around us provides a helpful lesson and guide in showing us the gifts that we all as individuals can bring to society – a glorious thing to contemplate.

Suminagashi

Suminagashi, or water marbling, is a Japanese marbling technique that dates back to the twelfth century. It translates as 'floating ink' and involves transferring the patterns created by the fluid motion on the water's surface onto paper, or some other kind of surface, like ceramic or fabric.

There is something meditative and calming about the process, particularly when you use more than one colour; the various different viscosities create patterns that seem to take on a life of their own.

1. Fill a pan or bowl with room-temperature water.

2. Using calligraphy ink or an oil-based ink, gently tap the surface of the water with the tip of a paintbrush a drop at a time, to see the ways in which the pigment interacts with the water. A high-quality pigmented ink will float on the water's surface; you can then create concentric circles, or gently allow the pigment to dissipate across the surface of the water, creating swirls and patterns by gently nudging the ink with a toothpick.

3. It's worth having some scrap paper to test with at first. Lay the surface of the paper (preferably uncoated, with a high gsm) on the water's surface, allowing for the print to transfer without it becoming submerged completely. You can also use this technique to print on ceramics, too. A thicker card or washi paper is ideal for making your creation a bit more robust and hardy – perfect for making gift labels, bookmarks and thank you cards.

4. Place your print on the side to dry, blotting gently with paper towels to aid the process if necessary.

Not only does the process beautifully capture the movement of water, but this practice was also called upon for its properties of divination. I spent one holiday season using the technique to create decorations for a tree, by using white ceramic stars and baubles to adorn my house with at Christmas time. The temporal nature of the activity and its ephemerality make it an ideal way to create cards at certain times of year, or to embellish fabric. It encourages you, through the fluidity of water, to navigate ideas of play and control – to become more confident and deft with movements the more you practice, while also surrendering yourself to the uncontrollable nature of the way the water and ink create patterns that cannot be repeated naturally.

Pressing, dyeing and printing with flowers

Although it's hard to compete with the scent and bloom of fresh flowers in the summertime, there is something charming and sentimental about repurposing flowers by extending their life further, particularly if they are from a bouquet that has a specific emotional meaning. The flower arrangements crafted for my wedding in late October were full of our favourite seasonal flowers and included foliage that had sentimental meaning for my family – ivy being part of my *kamon*, or Japanese family crest. Pressing and preserving flowers can capture and extend a joyful occasion or memory as a reminder to relish and find delight in these moments.

Some of my favourite methods involve pressing a flower (making sure it is dry) between two heavy books, nestled within two sheets of parchment or newspaper with the aid of a heavy weight. As a child, my biggest enemy was patience, particularly when it came to this process; for best results, it's worth waiting for between two to four weeks. However, depending on the conditions of your house (for example, if it is damp) it may take up to six weeks.

In a similar process to *suminagashi*, I also find that painting the petals of a flower, and gently using the pattern to print and stamp a canvas, is a lovely way of capturing its texture.

Another method I've used in the past involves extracting the natural dye from flower petals. For example, I once made a gift for a friend with one of the table settings after her wedding. On a silk

pillowcase, I lined up some of the different-coloured flowers before rolling the material into a sausage shape, with the petals inside. I then tied it securely with the use of colourless string (you can also use rubber bands), before boiling (or steaming, depending on how delicate the material you're using is) the whole thing in a pan of white vinegar and water (a ratio of 1:4) for about an hour or two. The end result is subtle and varied – some varieties of flowers, depending on the shape of the petal, can leave distinctive shapes, while others leave the faintest hue of pink or blue behind. Think tie-dye but muted and understated.

The Path Taken by Others

One of the ways in which I find comfort during times when I am creatively blocked comes from visiting museums and art galleries. My preference is always for the exhibitions that trace or focus on the work of a specific person – even if the style is not to my taste, there is something inherently universal about witnessing the output of a career in a way that no other path takes you. To see particular themes or techniques in an artist's work following a seismic change in their personal life, or to see the influence that their peers and contemporaries might have had and even – when witnessing the dates alongside particular works – to find times when they have taken a period of rest.

I find I engage with these spaces more effectively and receive the most benefit when visiting alone. It means I can create as much time as I need to focus on these places without judgement, making my visit as low pressure as possible. Whether I am engaging with art in particular or seeking out places for their therapeutic benefits, being able to do so without the pressure of having to perform for others has become part of my wellbeing practice.

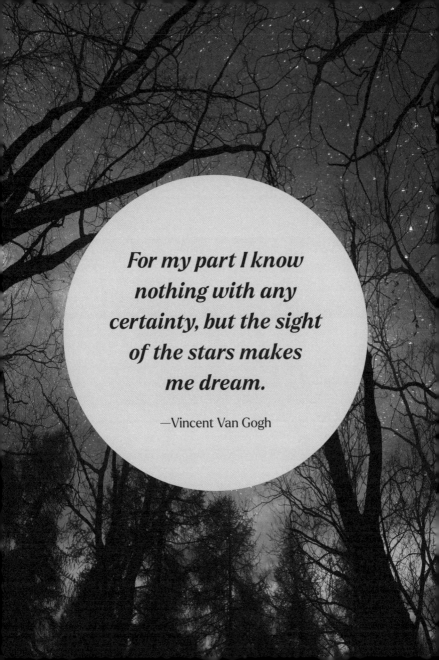

For my part I know
nothing with any
certainty, but the sight
of the stars makes
me dream.

—Vincent Van Gogh

Daily walks and wanders

A daily walk – a habit deemed necessary at first due to the addition of a family dog – is an endless source of wonder and an almost vital part of working through ideas and providing joy. With a curious mind, the practice provides a limitless supply of prompts: What was here before me? How did this get here? Why has that been put there? Some of these questions have led me on paths to discover the most fascinating things I had often previously walked straight past. The key is looking

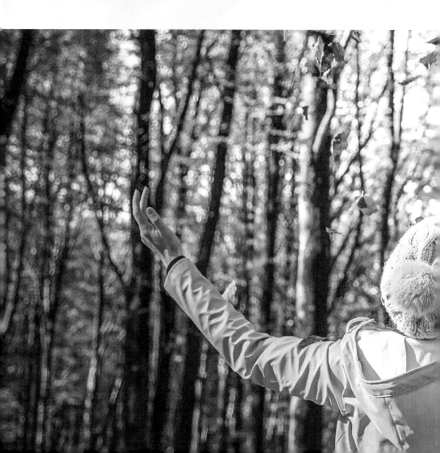

up, and around you. To wonder about the architects and craftspeople behind the buildings, perhaps the former residents of the homes. It was on one of these walks that I noticed what first appeared to be unsightly paint, a dark blemish that was decidedly out of place across the facade of the otherwise thoughtfully designed art deco town hall building. Following that thread of curiosity, I was delighted to later discover it to be camouflage paint, still present from the Second World War, the revelation providing me with the same sense of excitement

that I usually get from the plot of a thriller. Approach these walks inquisitively and actively, almost as if you are a tourist, savouring the time you get to discover and deepen your knowledge of your space.

The final destination does not have to be the objective – rather, it is about carving the time to allow for free-flowing thought, along with the benefits of movement and a change of scenery that can provide all the difference.

At a crossroads, we often share the old adage – *let nature take its course.* There is wisdom there for us to draw from – we just have to be open enough to see it.

On my walks, I have a greater sense of accountability through my pre-eminent chaperone, Milhouse, my excitable black-and-tan miniature dachshund. Knowing how much enjoyment he gets out of these rambles, and during an era where every dog walk can be mined for social media content, I am fiercely protective of this time, adamant to keep it as screen-free as possible – finding nourishment from the walk itself and enjoying the respite it provides while also keeping him out of mischief. Through our walks together, he often prompts me to touch and engage with things I hadn't before – different types of trees, for example – and I rarely come away from these walks without a new idea, a greater sense of feeling connected with my neighbourhood, or a respect and appreciation for the time of year we are in.

The accountable friend that I find in my canine companion is something I try to replicate in other areas of my life. In the same way that he finds wonder and has a desire to share his foraged joys (mostly of the stick variety), I try to make a practice and habit out of sharing the enchanting magic of my surroundings with those that I love. To be the person that someone can rely upon to give gentle reminders, and to offer whispered words of encouragement.

The benefits of these walks are not only in the physical: evidence supports the idea that physical activity can influence how we think,[3] and anecdotally how it can spark the imagination, allowing us to be mindful and conscious of noticing how we can help others (even if it is just putting bird feed out for the birds when pickings are slim).

These walks influence the way we think, but I find the impact is sustained further when I use it as subject matter, making mental notes and capturing the imperceptible changes to seek a new point of view.

Writing notes for your future self or adding things to your calendar as prompts can be a tender way of encouraging yourself, but I find the greatest comfort in the friends who share not just an artistic temperament but are also in careers that require a sense of risk and resilience. The physical act of writing a letter or inviting people to do something together – something creative, where the stakes are relatively low – can often be the perfect way of tackling a difficult subject.

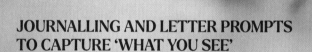

JOURNALLING AND LETTER PROMPTS
TO CAPTURE 'WHAT YOU SEE'

✻   How would you describe the branches of the trees?

✻   What plants, berries and flowers did you notice?

✻   How would you describe the colour of the sky?

✻   What do these sights evoke?

THE WONDROUS WORDS OF WINTER

Apricity: Describes the warmth of winter sun.

Hibernal: Relating to winter – from the Latin *hibernalis,* meaning 'wintry'.

Névé: Young, granular snow.

Firn: A Swiss-German word for last years' snow.

Rime: Frost, the type of opaque and granular ice particles that seem to coat and embellish in chilly conditions.

Tarot and Other Mystical Ways of Seeking New Perspectives

A weekly grounding ritual I partake in involves a set of well-worn tarot cards. Tarot reading has had a long and enduring history since the mid-fifteenth century and in modern times has enjoyed somewhat of a resurgence. Far from using the results of a particular reading to determine a course of action or depending on the outcome to manifest a particular situation, I use the reading as a time for myself, to reflect on where I am at a particular moment in time. I've found the ritual most effective when I do it for myself – the performative nature of a group reading can be somewhat distracting. The randomness and chance-based nature of the exercise often serve to call to mind an aspect of my life I might have neglected, or to find progress or abundance in an area I might have felt like I was lacking in. It can also be a healthy reminder to remain humble and show caution – gently advising you to slow down in areas you might be rushing into with reckless abandon. The element of ritual for me is important; I often light a candle and have a herbal tea, while thinking with intention and seeking a way to unpack an issue I might be dwelling over. In many ways, it feels like having a conversation with your intuition, the cards acting as a questioning friend. I find this a useful tool particularly when working over a creative idea, but one that I'm not quite ready to share yet.

Other tools I use for initiating creative conversations with my intuition involve tasseography – reading the patterns created by the sediment of tea leaves, coffee grounds or even in wine. I find a sense of beauty in its randomness and it can be a useful way of testing a new idea or working through a problem I'm struggling with – a useful first edit before taking an idea out to the wider world. Its mystical nature is part of its charm.

Tasseography and tarot: advice from a novice

The art of divination is really about becoming attuned to your sense of intuition. At least, this is a belief that I hold – that tasseography and tarot are useful tools for exploring concepts, rather than holding any psychic or mystical power of their own. To get the most out of it, start as you might a yoga practice – by setting your intention. Keep your mind focused on the questions and subjects you are seeking to explore as you go through the motions.

Tarot Reading: A good way to start is through a daily card pull, or perhaps a three-card spread. By shuffling the deck, you might place cards at random, face down, keeping your question or intention at the front of your mind before turning it over to reveal the answer. Of the seventy-eight cards in a deck, twenty-two are 'major arcana' and fifty-six are 'minor arcana' cards. The direction the cards are pointing, either upright or reverse, also has symbolism and relevance to your particular reading. Major arcana cards tend to deal in the wider, more overarching themes whereas minor arcana cards have a more temporal, fleeting meaning.

Traditional decks, like the Rider-Waite Tarot deck, can have some of their meanings and symbolism inferred by their illustrations and depending on which suits are represented. Wands might represent creativity and passion, whereas cups symbolize emotions; swords represent words and actions, while pentacles represent the material world, like our finances and career.

Tasseography: The interpretation of tea leaves – what the patterns reveal to and about the drinker – comes from first enjoying a cup of loose-leaf tea with intention (having the question in mind). The leaves that remain at the bottom of the cup can be interpreted in the same way you might make shapes out of clouds in the sky. There are various references to draw from, most notably a work on the subject written in the early twentieth century by an unnamed author with the enigmatic moniker 'A Highland Seer'.

INFUSING YOUR OWN TEAS

Creating your own herbal tea infusions is a lot simpler than you might imagine – there is something incredibly satisfying about doing so with the things you have grown yourself, as I have found when making calendula tea using the flowers from my modest inner-city garden. For an ideal herbal drink, I'd recommend a serving of about one tablespoon of dried herb for 250ml of water – double this ratio if you're considering using fresh herbs, as their steeped flavour won't be as strong as their dried counterparts. Rose, lavender and camomile are some of the more popular flowers you might find in your tea, but combining fresh and dried herbs with loose black tea can also be a nice gift for a loved one to usher in the winter season.

There is a real pleasure in creating your own blend – there's something luxurious about the bespoke combination of fresh and dried herbs. It's infinitely more satisfying when you take a zero-waste approach, by saving any citrus peelings that would have been otherwise discarded to incorporate as part of the process, too.

If you're lucky enough to be able to use homegrown herbs as part of your infusion, then the first step is to pick those herbs around dawn, before the sun fully rises, as some of the potency of the herb will be diffused by the sun's heat (which might scent your garden nicely but won't impart as much flavour in your cup). Dried herbs are much stronger than fresh herbs; you'll need about a third of the amount to get the same levels of flavour in your tea. To dry your own herbs, lay them out on some paper towel on a wire rack, rotating to ensure they dry fully; alternatively, brush off any stubborn dirt with a cloth before tying a bunch together and hanging upside down for a week or so (or once they are no longer moist). Whichever method you use, it's best to dry them out of direct sunlight, somewhere dry. You can also dry out your herbs and citrus peels by using a dehydrator (as I do), or in the oven on the lowest heat. To add a bit of dramatic flair, dry out flowers like hibiscus, lavender or rose.

When it comes to the blend itself, think of it as you might a perfume, one with a foundational base note, a complementary tone, and a powerful accent to set it off. Spices and roots like cinnamon, ginger and cardamom add a bit of flavour complexity. To make it a more traditional 'tea' as opposed to a tisane or herbal infusion, you can consider adding loose-leaf black or green tea to the mix.

Some of my home-crafted favourite blends include mint, sage and lemon or camomile, lavender and rose. Steep in water that is 95°C for around 3–5 minutes for dried ingredients, or 5–10 minutes if using fresh. Pour the tea through a strainer or by using a tea ball. My own interpretation of 'wintering' – the way I drew strength from those times when I sought out retreat and moments of peaceful tranquillity – came from a gentle opening of the mind. Keep your eyes open for the soft revelations that can come at times like these, whether through a contemplative walk or through play – in whatever form that takes for you. That might be a board game by a roaring fire, or gazing out the window with a cup of nourishing tea.

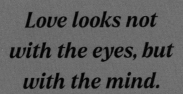

*Love looks not
with the eyes, but
with the mind.*

—William Shakespeare

Chapter 2

What to Listen Out For

How we can include ourselves and others

If you wish to know what most occupies a man's thoughts, you have only to listen to his conversation.

—Chinese Proverb

By the age of sixteen I had been in five different schools, a result of my father's profession as a diplomat. When I was growing up, a lot of my friends and acquaintances glamorized his career, and I often fielded questions from others looking to enter the foreign service. Besides being a talented linguist, however, my father was perhaps primed for the role due to his place in the family hierarchy. The youngest child and only son in a family with four siblings, for all his faults my father is a good and patient listener. Listening, reflecting and strategizing are his strengths, and he cut his teeth at home – with three talented, bright older sisters to learn from.

Often living in places where I was unfamiliar with the language or culture and battling an extreme shyness that stayed with me until my teenage years, I became used to listening. To recognizing the disconnect between what people said and what they did – but also to finding ideas that would sow themselves in my brain, to reap the rewards later.

Compassionate listening is an art I am trying to master. As a writer, an open and tuneful ear is vital – and yet we often are faced with a lot of rejection or vitriol or unsolicited opinions, capable of causing pain or a major setback. Striking the balance is close to impossible. Yet the times in my life where I have felt the most betrayed are when something comes to light that I would have perhaps been able to predict – and the betrayal is all the more painful as I feel keenly the sense of injustice I have done to myself, by second guessing.

Some of these lessons I learned the hard way, following the publication of my first book, *Japonisme*. It was a book shaped by my Japanese heritage and upbringing, a book focusing on wellbeing through the lens of the different cultural rituals, practices and traditions that I had grown up with. In it I had focused on the beauty

WHAT TO LISTEN OUT FOR

and majesty of the tea ceremony, flower arranging, forest bathing – all things shaped by my childhood in Japan. The book itself was largely drawn from a blog I had kept, six years of recipes, anecdotes and memories, a written record of the ways in which my cultural heritage had shaped my view on wellbeing and finding contentment. A lot of my childhood was distilled into that work – and so too was a sense of identity, one that I had worked through as someone with mixed heritage. Several things happened shortly after publication. First, that at a book launch to celebrate the event, a childhood friend arrived, completely drunk, with whole passages of the book crossed out in black marker. Despite not being a published writer himself, he felt the need to provide 'his edits and feedback' to my final product in front of an audience of peers, colleagues and friends. On the same night, my boyfriend at the time decided I needed to be 'taken down a peg', interrupting a conversation I was having with a journalist to inform me of the fact, before taking the opportunity to dump me in a mortifyingly public manner. My confidence was shattered. It was, I decided, my comeuppance for deciding to celebrate my achievement, which although to others may have seemed like a stroke of luck or an overnight success, had in fact taken close to a decade to accomplish. The final blow came from a comment on Amazon, a review that a distant acquaintance had found amusing and brought to my attention. A nameless, random commentator had shared that they liked the book, except for the places that 'this bitch kept banging on about her dead grandpa'. These events together created a sense of shame, of feeling perceived in ways that I felt particularly vulnerable about. The negative comments always endure more than the positive ones, in many ways, and only with the passage of time was I able to look back on those events as the lessons they were – in *how to listen*, *and what to listen to.* The most useful pieces of advice and feedback taught me something, while the ones coming from a place of fear and cruelty revealed more about where they originated than they did about me. Hindsight is a beautiful thing, and yet if I was able to write my first book again, the passages about my grandfather and the way that he shaped me would still be part of it. This comes only from understanding what to listen out for – to find the lessons where they are, but to practise self-compassion to separate the constructive from the cruelty, to listen attentively but to filter the noise.

Although much of what I write in this chapter requires a sense of hearing, it is not a prerequisite. It is more about having an openness of mind and heart and becoming attuned with the vibrations and frequencies of others and those around us. Some of the best listeners and the most perceptive people in my life are not able to hear – but have the most generous nature and open heart towards all the joys and pleasures of the universe. This is what I seek to cultivate further – to listen and act upon the messages from the universe, and those that stir within me.

In winter, we learn to embrace the silence that comes with a period of dormancy. Life can be chaotic, hurried and cacophonous – and this can cause us to lose our sense of self, as it becomes drowned out among all the noise. These quiet times of reflection allow us to connect more deeply with our feelings of intuition and observation – to pick up the muted notes of the little voice within you that does not need to shout to convey the truth.

The advantage of stillness is that it allows for meanings and values to come to the fore – a fact we often forget when we engage with opinions that differ from our own, particularly online. Negative comments are often amplified for a variety of reasons – humour,

perhaps, or controversy – but what drives engagement might not always be what is true or honourable, just noteworthy. When taking this in, these periods of rest are necessary to help keep a sense of distance and perspective – to collect our thoughts and ourselves, to align with our own beliefs and values before speaking out further. We have become so accustomed to fast responses and fast reactions that we lose sight of the fact that quicker isn't always better – consideration and care often require a slow, steady hand.

My first book was the result of several years of work, but also a lifetime of wrestling with my own mixed-race identity. The child of a Japanese mother and a British father, with one foot in each culture, I often felt that I didn't belong to either. As a child I yearned for a sense of identity and belonging that I felt I lacked. Writing a book in English about my Japanese upbringing and culture felt like a turning point.

Yet, on publication day, I felt a deep sense of humiliation and shame. Six years have passed between writing my first book, and writing this one, and *Japonisme* has been translated into close to twenty languages. Had I not spent that time crafting and working on myself, and let the pain flourish, I would not be able to continue as I have done. It is the time spent thinking, dreaming, listening that has helped me to understand the vital role that listening plays in this process. The quiet, fallow periods are necessary for the next crop.

What They Say, What They Mean

Feedback and constructive criticism are the fertilizers necessary for maturity and growth. They are uncomfortable, messy and you're often left wondering what is necessary, and what – for the lack of a more elegant description – is a load of horseshit. We are constantly bombarded with everyone's opinion, all the time, on absolutely everything, and if we are truly honest, not everyone is cut out to be a critic. Hanlon's Razor (the concept of not attributing to malice what can be attributed to stupidity) is a helpful tool but does not capture the complexity and nuance and the messiness of life. While it's tempting to dismiss everyone who disagrees with us as being stupid, it's simply not true and we must examine different perspectives to create something more lasting and integral. All this is much easier said than done – it's impossible not to feel defensive or protective, to take things personally and to defend your ideas in the realm of public opinion is exhausting.

A good friend might tolerate moments of bad behaviour, but a best friend will tell you – with love – when you're not doing yourself justice. It's the kindness in the message that is key, and this is often the missing ingredient that comes when you're able to freely share your opinion online, which can be cutting to the recipient and have no social consequences for the person spouting the vitriol.

It's a real challenge, finding the right balance. On one level, I often get an overwhelming urge to disengage, but many have careers and work that depend on being part of a wider conversation taking place online, and the reality is that in life we often have to deal with unwelcome conversations and observations that have the potential to shake our arguments and worldview. Even the most crudely worded criticisms have the potential to host something revelatory, or a flash of inspiration – like finding truffles in the muck.

For me, the medium is the message – and I've taken an 'easy come, easy go' approach. A comment on a post, filled with personal attacks and hate, which might have taken fifteen seconds to write, I try to dismiss – these are clearly written in flashes of uncontrollable anger. I may feel the need to be in control, to feel satiated, but it is a hollow form of release – unsatisfying, unhealthy and draining. I try to match the energy, which is easier said than done, but if a comment took fifteen seconds to write, then I'll give it the same amount of time in my head. Working through feedback with those that challenge and spar with you, rather than those who blindly agree with everything you say, is invaluable.

In order to become resilient, however, you cannot underestimate the necessity of proactively building in time for self-compassion and care during these moments. The terrain is filled with obstacles – emotional and physical trauma to work through, navigating a landscape filled with landmines you didn't even know were lurking under the surface. It is complex work – and complex work requires the release of pain through play.

Finding Our Flow

How often do we dedicate the time to protect, cherish and check in with our own hopes, dreams and desires? To carve out a period to reflect? We might unknowingly be more conscious of the wishes and needs of our partners, children, colleagues and friends than we might be of our own. The mere concept of focusing on our own thoughts without dwelling on the needs of others, or to put ourself first in this way, might feel so uncomfortable that it becomes something we dread, akin to making excruciating small talk at a tedious cocktail party.

Becoming in touch with our subconscious – by keeping an ear out for those vital clues – is often much simpler when you find focus and productivity by achieving a state of deep focus, or by getting in the flow.

Resilience can be built and worked through by finding ways to become in the thrall of a state of flow. This might be where your sense of awareness is tied to a specific action, albeit one that requires some amount of challenge or skill to keep you occupied. For me, this comes from cooking – the type of spontaneous, store-cupboard experimentation that requires no precision in measuring and is based on tactile cues rather than from looking at the clock. For my husband, I often see him enter this state while he's playing his video games – a welcome release from a hectic shift.

One outlet, perhaps, could be through exploring textiles and texture. I often 'unstick' my creative blocks by focusing on utilizing other parts of my brain – either through activities like knitting and sewing or other crafts like sculpting and painting – to work through these challenges. My Japanese grandfather would often find solutions to problems he faced at work through creative pursuits like flower arrangement or gardening, and often the sensations triggered by different textures and muscle memory can provide insight and activate

pathways left dormant otherwise. I often find it beneficial to have hobbies and interests that you do purely for the joy of the process, rather than the outcome (and anyone who is waiting on receiving a lumpy jumper from me can attest to that).

Meditative and repetitive activities, like knitting or crochet, are two things that help you to exercise a level of patience that we often don't practise or prioritize in the day to day. I'm not a believer that people can be innately good at these things – there's no way around it other than putting the hours in, and knowing this can be developed over time is immensely satisfying once you finally manage to complete a project that has been gathering dust in your desk. The sensation of doing something tactile also allows my mind to wander, seeing new patterns and images in a way that I am not able to without giving myself the space. I like to think of it as 'meditation-lite' – a gateway for those who find deeper meditation more challenging because they are addicted to being in a more 'productive' state, something that many of those around me seem to be afflicted with.

The best activities to trigger this kind of state come from those that have a resolution of one kind – the end of a crossword puzzle, perhaps.

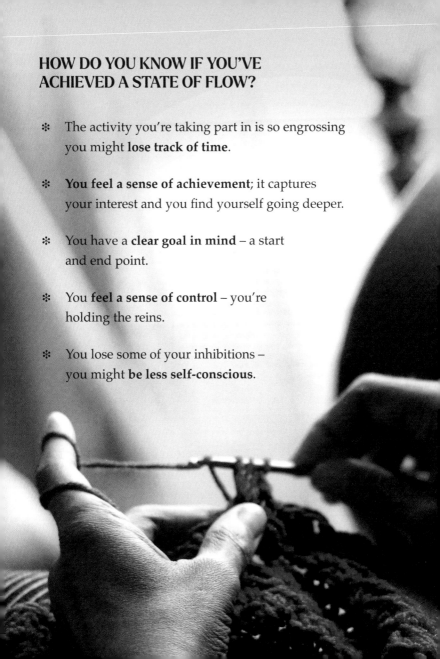

HOW DO YOU KNOW IF YOU'VE ACHIEVED A STATE OF FLOW?

❋   The activity you're taking part in is so engrossing
    you might **lose track of time**.

❋   **You feel a sense of achievement**; it captures
    your interest and you find yourself going deeper.

❋   You have a **clear goal in mind** – a start
    and end point.

❋   You **feel a sense of control** – you're
    holding the reins.

❋   You lose some of your inhibitions –
    you might **be less self-conscious**.

Some suggestions for flow state activities

Try to think about what you enjoyed as a child or adolescent: did you have a particular hobby that you've lost touch with? Try to remember that the flow state is not about a finished product, it's simply about the act of *doing*, so if you used to draw or paint but think you will no longer be any good at it – try it anyway, you might surprise yourself!

* Do a jigsaw puzzle.
* Try some gentle gardening – indoor or outdoor.
* Tackle an interior design project – from rearranging your shelves to painting a wall, this can be creative and rewarding with little effort.
* Practise a musical instrument, singing or even dancing to your favourite album.
* Try a new physical activity, like rock climbing or swimming.
* Start a new craft project.
* Cook a meal from scratch.

Who Is It For?

If looking out for inspiration has resulted in an idea for a creative project, then the listening phase is about understanding who it's for – those who will be receiving it, and who are also part of the conversation. Perhaps you wish to deepen the connection with those around you. Active, conscious listening is so readily forgotten, particularly for those who struggle to assert themselves, or fear they will be misunderstood. This stage will require you to listen actively, with sympathy and empathy. To put yourself in the place of others, to listen out for a rhythm or a melody, and trying to keep time. It is vital at this stage to keep schtum and listen. Soak it in, inform and feed your idea, giving yourself the time to think before speaking, because that will come later. It is the time to come up with the theories you'll be testing out; experiment with formats, work the clay a little before your idea takes its final form. What is the thing that I want to see most in the world? What can I do for others? The answers to these questions can come not by asking more questions, but by letting the answers come to you in the silence – or from the actions of others.

To do all the talking and not be willing to listen is a form of greed.

—Democritus

The joy of wintering, above all, is about choosing a slower and more considered pace. To see tranquillity and abundance in peace, and to find comfort in the silences. To consider new and rich perspectives by de-centring your ego or self, allowing yourself to become a conduit and receiver. The work of Pauline Oliveros with regard to 'deep listening' resonates here – to draw upon what is being said, combined with non-verbal cues, and a generous and empathetic desire to understand the frame of reference from which others may view the world. We all have a unique way of understanding the world around us; these quiet periods provide us ample opportunity from which to consider perspectives beyond our own narrow imaginations.

Sound-based Rituals

For many years I played the cello, an instrument that for a person my size was quite cumbersome (I never grew into a full-sized instrument, and to this day a ⅞-sized cello is gathering dust in my mother's house). I gave it up once I left school, the appeal for me fading without the draw of my closest friends in the orchestra with me. Yet it was through my time playing the cello that the impact of periods of silence and rest became apparent – the periods of rest captured in the musical notation allowing for the sound to reverberate further, or allowing me to hear the harmonies provided by the violas and violins, or even just to allow me to collect myself to have a greater impact at a later time. Any musician, or simply those who find joy and escape in listening to music, know that rest and space within music can allow for the sound to be sustained – creating moments of beauty and reflection.

From my days in the school orchestra, my favourite part was always the sense of ritual and routine, particularly around becoming *in tune* with one another. There was unpacking our instruments, applying the resin to our bows, but nothing felt more like a group of individuals coming together to work towards a common goal than when we began to tune our instruments together. Once the tuning fork provided the pitch, it would signal a change in shift – joking, playful students suddenly focusing on the task at hand, together.

Tuning forks are often used in alternative medicine for the purported benefits in finding a specific frequency, which supposedly has healing properties. For myself, this might be psychosomatic, but I do find comfort in a ritual when I approach my creative practice that involves a cleansing sound. Before I sit down to write in the mornings, I often write three pages of freehand journalling to clear

Try to be in good company, even when you are alone.

—Hungarian Proverb

my head, but what precedes this is a type of purification ritual for my desk, no doubt shaped by my East Asian upbringing. The lit candle, watering of plants, followed by the sound and humming of tapping a tuning fork on my desk, provides me with a moment of reflection, a metaphorical cleansing of the slate before I begin to shift my focus towards the writing task I have at hand.

Similar benefits from times I've required a deeper sense of healing come from attending and participating in **sound baths**. I've found these helpful as they are not self-directed, but often involve you either lying down or being seated in a comfortable position while the sounds wash over you – whether it's through using a gong, an ocean drum or a rainstick. The different frequencies help to provide a space for contemplation, allowing for different emotions and thoughts to rise to the surface. Sound baths often employ the use of gongs, crystal

bowls, bells and Tibetan singing bowls that have a resonating and deeply reverberating effect. The bells and bowls are often considered spiritually to have the power to alter a person's state – to evoke and encourage a feeling of internal harmony.

Another beautiful reminder of the ephemeral nature of the world around us comes from the use of **wind chimes**, which is also influenced by my childhood in Japan. They are often placed in gardens and in sacred places as a reminder of the constant flow of life, to check in with your environment and yourself – a delicate way of marking the passage of time.

The stillness, recovery and reflection process of wintering can be aided by the use of sound therapies of this kind.[4] Whether as an aid to meditation, or to help to release tension, there is something incredibly moving about lying supine while feeling the sound envelop and almost move through your entire being.

> Many countries throughout Europe have a winter bell ringing tradition, but the folk custom of Zvončari in Rijeka, Croatia is perhaps one of the most notable and moving. A tradition with pagan origins, shepherds don costumes and parade in villages with the ultimate aim of driving away the evil spirits of winter to bring forth the spring.

Intentional Listening, and How We Can Cultivate More of It in Our Lives

An artform that we, as a society, will always need to improve, work at, and build upon is the art of conversation. Perhaps it is more to do with the way technology is evolving, or perhaps we are still recovering from a period of isolation following a tumultuous few years caused by a global pandemic, but often people seem to be simply waiting for their 'turn' to speak rather than actively listening to the other person, honing in on a key word to allow them to wax lyrical instead of trying to deepen their knowledge of a particular topic or better understand their conversation partner. This is even more true when you know someone well – your perception of them is based on knowing them as they were at a particular moment in time, or in relation to you. It's the most infuriating thing about engaging

with our parents and grandparents, for example – who remember that you love the colour blue, or have a sweet tooth, even if your tastes and opinions have changed and adapted since. I'm especially guilty of this when it comes to my partner, making assumptions about his choices and behaviour when in fact the thing I love about him the most is his willingness to try new things, to hear other opinions and be shaped by them.

In my life, I try to cultivate this by asking questions to drive the conversation forward – to try and understand the other person's character and worldview. Whenever I get my hair cut, for example, I often ask the stylist if they were stuck on a desert island, what tool and product would they take with them, and why. Or, if my partner is frustrated by an aspect of his day, I ask what his impression of the actions of others might have been. The *why* questions are more revealing than the *what* or *how* questions and are a helpful way of dispelling your preconceptions – or affirming them. They help to strengthen relationships and build closeness, but also provide endless inspiration for sparking creativity.

It's why I'm also a big proponent of the voice note when keeping in touch with friends and loved ones. Unlike a phone call, which can take up a lot of time or take a while for schedules to align, or a text-based message, which often leaves much to interpretation, soliciting a voice note is like asking a friend to take the stage. It requires you to pay attention – to focus on them, and not yourself, but also so much can be gleaned from the pauses and hesitations that can get overlooked in day-to-day conversations. It forces you into the role of therapist, in many ways, and I find it such a useful tool – particularly when it comes to giving thoughtful, measured and meaningful reassurances in return.

True friendship does not freeze in the winter.

—German Proverb

Sounds come alive in the summer – the cacophony of birdsong, the melodic humming of insect life, the raucous laughter and joy from street parties, barbecues, sport. It is abundant and everywhere; as a result, I find it an absolute nightmare trying to get anything done in the summer periods of my life. The stillness and muted quiet times of winter are the optimal times to focus – to listen out for the softly spoken pearls of wisdom from the voice that comes from within.

Compassionate voices are often crucial for a creative project in its infancy. Sharing an idea too early, can often create a hostile environment before the idea has even begun to take root – and particularly for those who are risk averse, it is often done not out of spite, but a misplaced sense of love. Creative play is not logical and you may need to find the space to cultivate the sapling of an idea that may not be hardy enough to withstand the biting frost of judgement. Following the publication of my first book, I made the mistake of sharing ideas I had, or was excited about, only for others to recommend other books on a similar topic, or to suggest that the tide might have turned, that things were 'overdone' or 'cliched' and were therefore discarded and abandoned. Yet these voices, well-intentioned as they may be, are often driven by fear rather than love. Of a desire to protect in safety, rather than risk the scrapes and bruises that come from play. So once you have a creative idea, sit with it a while; let it simmer, and during this time of listening with intention add to it – a sprinkle of this, a dash of that – but let it mature and develop in silence and grace. The sharing part comes later – now is the time to listen to yourself, before seeking the opinions of others.

Chapter 3

What We Touch
How we can capture our ideas

*To appreciate the beauty of a
snowflake it is necessary to
stand out in the cold.*

—Aristotle

When we find ourselves in a state of disbelief or uncertainty, we reach out to touch – just to make sure. It was the sensation I craved the most during my time in lockdown, and it was only when, after five months of not touching another person, that the magnitude of what was occurring registered to me. Until then I had been in a state of detachment and only when I was back with my partner after five months of being apart did all the emotions and the fear I had been dealing with flood through my body, which had until that time been in a state of dreamlike suspension.

The blistering heat, the biting cold – and the contrast between the two, as well as the shades of sensation in between – have a visceral potency that helps to ignite the creative senses. 'Contrast therapy' – where an individual might follow a bracing cold-water swim with the warmth of a sauna, and back again – has swelled in popularity, due to its capacity to release endorphins and its benefits for our cognitive function and circulatory systems.[5] For me, it's a trusted and tested way to kick-start and reset when I'm at an impasse. A way to get out of my head, and back into the room. Studies conducted at Maastrict University have also shown that those exposed to colder temperatures have improved levels of focus, attention and reaction times – ideal for when you're looking to dispel those cobwebs.[6]

Archimedes supposedly had his 'eureka' moment in the bath, the place where I have had several moments of clarity of my own – but the most reliable way of inspiring these moments and pearls of wisdom come, for me, when changing states – when leaving the comfort of my warm living room to drag the dog around the drizzly downs, or plunging from a sun-kissed deck into a body of ice-cold water. When following a thread of an idea, I often find myself undressing, and then re-dressing – discarding a frayed

*To touch the earth
is to have harmony
with nature.*

—Native American
Oglala Sioux Proverb

bathrobe for a woollen jumper, which in turn gets discarded as I find myself in the passionate throes of a new idea, which makes the jumper feel constricting.

Once we have received an idea, and considered the perspective of others, then it is through touch that we begin to realize its full potential. The phrase 'touchstone' comes from a physical tool, used to test precious metal alloys to determine their authenticity or purity. In the same way, the sense of touch can be used not only to test an idea, but also to propel an idea forward, or kick-start creativity when you're feeling stuck.

When something doesn't 'feel right', I find it to be a type of spirit level or gauge for my intuition. Our perception is guided by the eyes and ears, but it is the sensation of touch that provides the heft, security and authority to drive the confidence to make a decision or move forward with a particular idea or project. Touching something gives a sense of legitimacy, of being tangible, and while you are at a stage of ideation, being aware of your physicality both as a barometer but also as a way of keeping attuned can be incredibly beneficial.

I often think of creative ideas as though they were something buoyant; there is a limitless supply, but you do have to keep an open mind in order to receive them. To bring them to life or to provide substance is the challenge – and that is what we do through touch. Perhaps we moor them together and anchor them in some way; this is how we bring these ideas to the notice of others, by capturing them somehow. Whether it is through words or through painting, knitting or sculpture, it is through touch that we contain it – touch as action. The idea is the easy part.

Any author will tell you that when you publish your first book, countless individuals in your life will suddenly appear, telling you that they too have an idea for a book. Every person has a book inside them, and the only difference between someone with *an idea* for a book and someone with a finished book is that the latter has captured their idea somehow in a way transmissible to others. Whether you have a book inside you, or some form of creative passion you are looking to share, it is through the sense of touch that you must capture it, to set it free. The sense of touch is how we *physically* create; in this chapter I explore the ways in which we can ignite and harness the power of the mind–body connection. Sight and sound are how we take things in, but touch is how we express ourselves. When we feel disconnected from our own wishes and desires, we often imagine ourselves as being misaligned, or out of sync. Through movement, heat and texture we practise maintaining that connection on a physical and spiritual level.

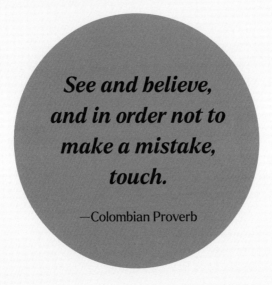

See and believe, and in order not to make a mistake, touch.

—Colombian Proverb

The Cold: Ice Baths and Cold-water Swimming

No experience is perhaps as humbling and life-affirming as plunging yourself into a body of ice-cold water, but it is the most action-oriented way to inspire thought – even if those thoughts are *Why am I doing this to myself?* If the full-body plunge is unattainable or a bit less convenient, morning 'ice facials' have seen a surge in popularity: running a cube of ice first thing across your face to awaken the body and mind.

Ice facials

I particularly enjoy an ice facial first thing in the morning to reduce puffiness, using a flannel or a pair of exfoliating gloves to hold a piece of ice so I can run it deftly along my skin. The process is incredibly calming and meditative, particularly when using a chunky piece of ice, which can be achieved by using moulds made specifically for the purpose of administering an ice facial, or the type of ice-cube tray built for making the perfect Old-fashioned whisky cocktail.

Always working in an upward motion, going from the inside towards the outside of your face, you can run the ice cube above your eyebrows, across your cheekbones and from your chin up towards your ears. For best results, you should always do this with clean skin, followed by your usual skincare routine.

Immersing yourself in cold water

Cold water swimming is one of those activities where the biggest challenge is committing to it in the first place. The last thing I want to do, surely, is take myself out of a place of comfort, and deliberately send my body into fight or flight mode – and yet nothing captures or can evoke a sense of euphoria quite like it, in such a short period of time.

Having spent a considerable part of my childhood in Japan, where *onsen* or hot spring culture pervades, it's common to go from different states: from a bubbling, hot sulphuric spring straight into an ice bath to cool off. I learned from a young age that the way to do it involves mind over matter; that once you're in it up to your neck, you can begin to enjoy it. Which is a metaphor for life, in many ways. It's also a reminder that it's always good to be prepared, whether by having the proper gear, like a neoprene suit, or having a hot drink, a proper robe and towels close by to dry off. Always do any cold-water swimming in the company of others. Many Nordic countries share a tradition of ice swimming, handed down from generation to generation as a sense of building community and a way of stimulating your body – and those endorphins, too.

The Heat: Saunas

The happiest country in the world, according to the World Happiness Report,[7] is Finland – where ice swimming often goes hand in hand with a long-standing appreciation of the sauna, part of their intangible cultural heritage. The spirit of the sauna, or *löyly*, is said to reside in the stones, and is released once water is poured over them, revealed as the steam.

In contrast to the biting and bracing cold of an ice swim, being enveloped in the heat and humidity can provide relief to a tired body and restless mind. When you swim in cold water, your mind has a razor-like focus on the shock that is taking place across the body; stilling the mind in the sauna requires a bit more concentration.

To aid this, I often turn to one of two visualizations. The first is for growth, when I am looking to create a mindset of abundance, and involves seeing myself as a little piece of dough rising and baking in an oven. What I become depends on where my mind is going that day (sometimes I'm a croissant, other days I'm a loaf of bread) but focusing on that visual image helps to clear my mind of the mental clutter. The other visualization is for release – if I am looking to let something go, whether it's a grudge or something that is no longer serving me to hold onto. In this case, the visual crutch I use is that I am a scoop of ice cream, melting slowly into the beach, becoming part of the sand, sea and into the infinite horizon.

The fire is winter's fruit.

—Arabian Proverb

WHAT WE TOUCH

Movement for Inspiration and Healing

I consider myself an incredibly emotional person, given that my parents, by many standards, are not from cultural backgrounds that actively encourage outward displays of emotion. I am moved to tears easily but was often made to suppress my emotional outbursts as a child; as an adult I struggle to express myself without feelings of guilt and shame. The result of this is that for several years of my life I went into relationships in a detached way, either through moving countries every three years or through a latent sense of fear of abandonment. I approached most relationships with a sense of distance, constantly preparing an exit route or avoiding commitment at all costs. This left me ill-equipped to deal with the messiness of life, particularly when it came to dealing with loss and grief.

My yoga practice is what gave me the space and the tools to begin to unpack and process these emotions. What I was not able to comprehend logically, I was able to physically – whether it was through an energetic vinyasa practice, or through leaning into a sense of stillness, with a series of movements inspired by a yin yoga approach.

The first stage of healing – for me – is movement, whether that is coming out of a period of creative blockage or trying to process some difficult or challenging news. By stretching my body in a different way, new channels make themselves known to me – both conscious and unconscious. By placing my hands on the ground, I find new connections and different ways of breathing stoke new ideas, like glowing embers on a fire.

I started my personal process in classes with other people, as many do. But with time, my practice has become more solitary – less self-conscious, more as a way to tap into my own wellbeing. My yoga practice is another way of incorporating touch in my life, along with daily walks.

Yoga for strength, rest and healing

The adaptability of yoga as a discipline is what keeps me consistently coming back to the mat. As long as you show up, it can be as challenging/gruelling/compassionate/nurturing as you need it to be. As an activity, it is flexible and adaptable and is therefore an endless resource for development and working through the challenges we face, both physically and emotionally.

Working through different stages and types of asana, or body postures, reflect the cyclical nature of life, the changing seasons, and the universe; through the various flows and actions we build resilience and test our boundaries, but also prioritize rest (shavasana) in equal measure. Rest and reflection, gratitude and patience are also an integral part of a holistic yoga practice; the emotional benefits we get from a physical practice of this kind are nothing short of extraordinary.

Following the thread

I try to capture the senses and memories evoked by the sense of touch as part of my creative writing process by getting it *down*. This is often by taking pen to paper, but sometimes it takes the form of a smattering of voice notes, or a few jottings in my notes app. Movement, and the memories evoked by the different textures throughout the day, usually take a little while to create meaning; it is only through a period of reflection, and with the benefit of hindsight and time that I can begin to connect the dots together. Getting it down – whether it is through freehand writing or recording a stream of consciousness for yourself to reflect upon later – helps to make the intangible tangible. Getting something down in writing always adds an element of legitimacy, and keeping a record allows you to come back to it, to follow your previous train of thought. Following the thread will allow you to visualize and create a beautiful woven tapestry.

This can be achieved through journalling, perhaps prompted by a record for posterity of the natural world in its wintrous state, or through manifestation, gratitude or free-form as a way to process and more clearly understand your emotional state.

Sometimes, the physical act of converting our thoughts to written words – the process of it – can help to lighten and alleviate. A study at Penn State University showed that patients who journalled had fewer depressive symptoms, were more resilient and less anxious after incorporating the habit of positive journalling over a period of time.[8] Negative thought patterns can be hard to break out of and journalling is one tool that we can use to break these down and address them in an action-oriented way.

There are days where it is simply more cathartic to use my journalling time as a place to rant or wallow – to let my worries spill out across the page. Most days, I try to focus on prompts that encourage a mindset of where I'd like to be – a strong, positive place. These might include:

* What are my strengths?
* What do I enjoy?
* What am I grateful for?
* What small changes can I commit to?
* What do I need to practise?

The journalling process allows me to tangibly work through these, providing much benefit, but for areas that I find to be more blocked than others, it can be the catalyst to spur me into action.

THE MEMORIES IMPARTED BY
TOUCH – SOOTHING THE STING

Our senses respond and react to the slightest of injuries and the effects can be lingering and sustained.

I was stung by a bee, once. Close to twenty years have passed since that moment, but my body still remembers the sensation so vividly, mostly because it came at a time completely unexpected. I'd spent years of my life tempting fate, running unscathed through the rotting and overripe fruit that had fallen from the trees in my grandparents' orchard, and yet I felt the sharp, bitter pain of the tiny creature as it stung my chin in the unlikeliest of places: the scented candle section of a luxury department store.

The kind shop assistants were mortified. I was affronted; it felt so bizarrely out of context, this solitary bee in these plush surroundings (on the fourth floor of the building). There was no explanation as to how it had got there, why it had chosen to go for me; there was nothing in the employee handbook to offer a solution. Yet it served as a stark reminder of the unpredictability of the creative process – that sharp pains and jabs can really come when you least expect it – but also the ways in which we impact others clumsily, without noticing. That our seemingly insignificant movements can shake other beings to the core, driving them to drastic action. What we touch can also touch us, in a ripple effect. Our responsibility – should we choose the path of kindness and to act with compassion – is to never forget that fact. To show strength and mettle when we need to, but not to renounce our tenderness and humanity in the process.

The sting felt like a needle, but lingered and burned, swelling over the next few hours. The swelling matured into aching, an

emotional weight as well as physical pain.

On the cusp of puberty, I was constantly provoking myself into one of two states – rapid anger or a sense of despair. In this instance I felt a great deal of sadness, for the confused and lost little creature, led astray no doubt by a plethora of enticing smells, only to find itself in danger.

This memory reminds me of the way we build resilience: through self-care, building up tolerance, learning lessons for the future. The memory was a formative one, one of the earliest in which I encountered a sensation I had perhaps only read about before.

Shiatsu, Tapping and Massage

Shiatsu, or Japanese finger pressure technique, is a form of acupressure massage treatment where a practitioner applies pressure to certain points (known as *tsubo*) to facilitate the flow of 'ki' or 'chi' energy in the body. The objective is to provide relief and soothe ailments and tension caused by blockages of 'ki'. This is done through kneading, holding, pressing, tapping and stretching the body without the use of instruments.

Similar principles can be seen in 'EFT tapping', otherwise known as 'emotional freedom tapping', a technique that helps practitioners draw mindful awareness to their body and breathing when processing trauma or complex feelings and emotions.

When I would struggle to fall asleep as a child, or be fretful or nervous, my mother always used to lightly tap the centre of my forehead (what some call their 'third eye' in yoga), and the result was often incredibly comforting and soothing.

To get the benefit of tapping, one might lightly tap themselves:

* ❉ On the top of their head
* ❉ Between the brows
* ❉ By their temples
* ❉ Under their eyes, or at the top of their cheekbones
* ❉ On their top lip
* ❉ On the chin
* ❉ At the top of the collarbone
* ❉ Under each arm

For simple stress relief

Place your hands on either side of your head, with your fingers on the scalp and your thumbs by your temples. Breathing deeply, rotate your thumbs in a circular motion.

For sleeplessness

Using your right thumb and index finger, press between and along the thumb and index finger of the left hand repeatedly, pulsing along (your left hand should be in the shape of the letter 'c').

For relaxation

Using both hands, press along and across the soles of your feet, focusing on each foot individually.

It is through touch that we bring our vision to others. We see, we hear – and from here, we create. Paint to canvas, pen to paper – this is the act of getting it down, and out there. For many years, I kept a diary for this purpose, a record for myself. Through touch we give and receive, tapping into a reservoir of creative energy. This is the easy part; this is the place that feels safe. When we've been through a period of trauma we crave this comfort, and so it is better – and beneficial – for us to stay here.

However, there comes a time when 'safe' becomes dangerous. When a pond, beautiful in its stillness, begins to appear stagnant. Unsavoury. Inert. Fear can set in at this stage, and it feels all-consuming, so you do nothing, say nothing, feel nothing. You feel nothing, and nothing feels you. You touch nothing, and therefore you do not create any change, add anything – positive or negative. This isn't what we are made for – we need to reach out. Grab it by the horns, put those feelers out, put your nose to the grindstone. Get it down, first, and then – and only when you're ready – get it out there.

Chapter 4

How We Breathe
Sharing our journey with others

For breath is life, and if you breathe well you will live long on earth.

—Sanskrit Proverb

As a child, I used to suffer from the types of nightmares that would leave me with sleep paralysis: my mind would be awake and I would be able to see what was going on, but I would be unable to move, trapped in a fearful dream. These occurrences were infrequent but left me with a sense of trepidation and fear around bedtime – the usual nighttime ritual of *getting ready for bed* instilling dread rather than comfort. My poor sleep-deprived parents must have despaired over this phenomenon. As a result, I'd attempt to put off sleep by reading through the night, stashing torches under my pillow and a selection of books in order to stave off this feeling for as long as possible.

I still remember it vividly – the feelings of helplessness and isolation, caused by fear and anxiety but exacerbated by panicked and shallow breathing. The turning point came for me one summer when I confided in my grandfather, Haruyuki, who coaxed it out of me – the feeling I was so afraid of, the ways in which I would try to hold off the release of sleep as long as possible, and how the cycle felt infinite, inevitable, enduring.

My grandfather was an incredibly successful and driven businessman, but also a deeply spiritual person. He held close a set of rituals in his routine, outlets for play and creativity, even in a life that in many ways felt heavily scheduled and prescriptive. So perhaps it is not surprising that it is through him I learned the way to overcome the fear at the root of my sleep paralysis – through chanting '*Nam Myōhō Renge Kyō*' – a devotion to the law of the lotus sutra. He taught me the chant – which I could run through my mind, even if I wasn't capable of verbalizing it – as a way to rebalance negative karma, a tool to draw comfort through the repetition of the chant. Its meaning, revealed to me by my grandfather, was that the chant serves to remind us that we have the power within us all, innately, to transform

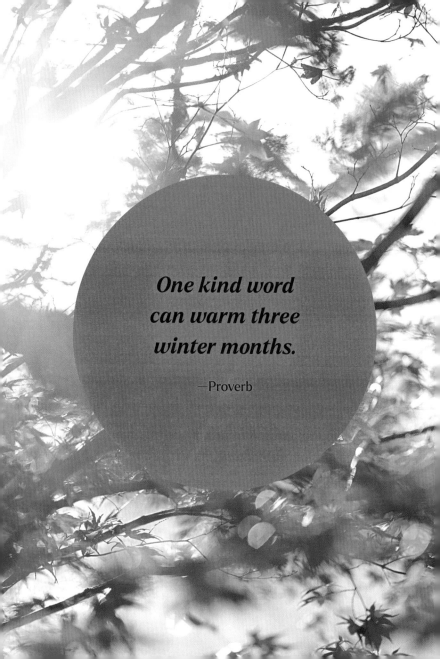

One kind word
can warm three
winter months.

—Proverb

and overcome all suffering. That we are able to call upon that strength, both internally and externally, whenever we need. That in order to deeply hold the chant I must breathe in through my nose and hold the breath in the base of my stomach – but that breathing with intention was the most crucial part of all.

Shōdai is the practice of prolonged chanting in Nichiren Buddhism and is something I draw upon very rarely, only in times of real distress. But breathing with intention, whether it is sharing a kind word, asking for help or doing meditative breathing, is something I've found myself turning to again and again. How we breathe, and the way we use our breath to communicate and speak – whether it is sharing our thoughts and ideas with others or finding the strength and courage to do so – requires bravery and intentionality.

Countless studies have been conducted to support the neurophysiological benefits of chanting; for others, a similar effect is achieved through prayer.

An unsettled and anxious mind makes its displeasure known throughout the body – your breathing becomes more rapid, yet shallow – taking the entire system down with it. Becoming mindful of this fact can be incredibly helpful – a way in which to centre and ground yourself. A swimmer, about to dive into a pool, takes in a deep breath to allow themselves to propel further, to sustain being underwater for a longer period of time. A similar principle can be considered here. After a period of reflection, contemplation and exploration, we might begin to venture and share our own thoughts and perspectives.

We breathe year round, but for those of us who reside in colder climates our awareness is perhaps more deeply drawn to it in the winter, the chill serving to illuminate a misty cloud, perhaps, during a time of year when we have to wrap up to keep warm outside.

By bringing conscious awareness to our breathing, we can work to build it at a level that is deeper and richer. Perhaps by doing so, it can serve to develop the ways in which we use our breath to share and build connections. In doing so, we can help ourselves to navigate even the most inclement personal seasons and circumstances.

Sharing Our Creations with Others

Without a doubt this is the scariest part of the creative process, but no pain, no gain. Ever since I can remember I've kept a diary, but the serendipitous turn of events which led to my first book came only after I stopped keeping my thoughts, recipes and perspectives to myself and put it out there, on a blog, for the whole world to see. It provided a great deal of amusement and ribbing from friends, as well as those who were not so charitably minded . . . and yet, this is the risk we must take if we are going to be our most honest and authentic selves. We must run the risk of being laughed at, or made fun of, or shot down and rejected. Once we've managed to get our idea *down*, we've got to get it out *there* – and I'm afraid in order to do that, we need to share, just like we learned to do as children.

If you're still working through an idea, find a trusted and receptive audience first – there's nothing more devastating than having an idea ripped apart by someone who might misunderstand it, or who isn't the audience it was intended for. When you have worked through an idea and are more confident, then at this later stage you will be able to weather any criticism – this feedback, if true, will provide the most vital growth for you as a creative.

ASKING FOR HELP

I'm still unbelievably terrible at this, but in this instance do as I say not as I do – *ask for help*. Use your words to find support, show vulnerability, seek empathy. If you need it, ask for it. The risk is often negligible, but the reward too great not to take that risk.

WINTER SOLSTICE AND THE YULE LOG

Winter solstice traditions have their roots in pagan fire customs, and have been adapted throughout various regions, each with their own unique cultural and social history. The burning of the yule log, which served to provide light and warmth, also brought with it the tradition of storytelling and bringing people closer together.

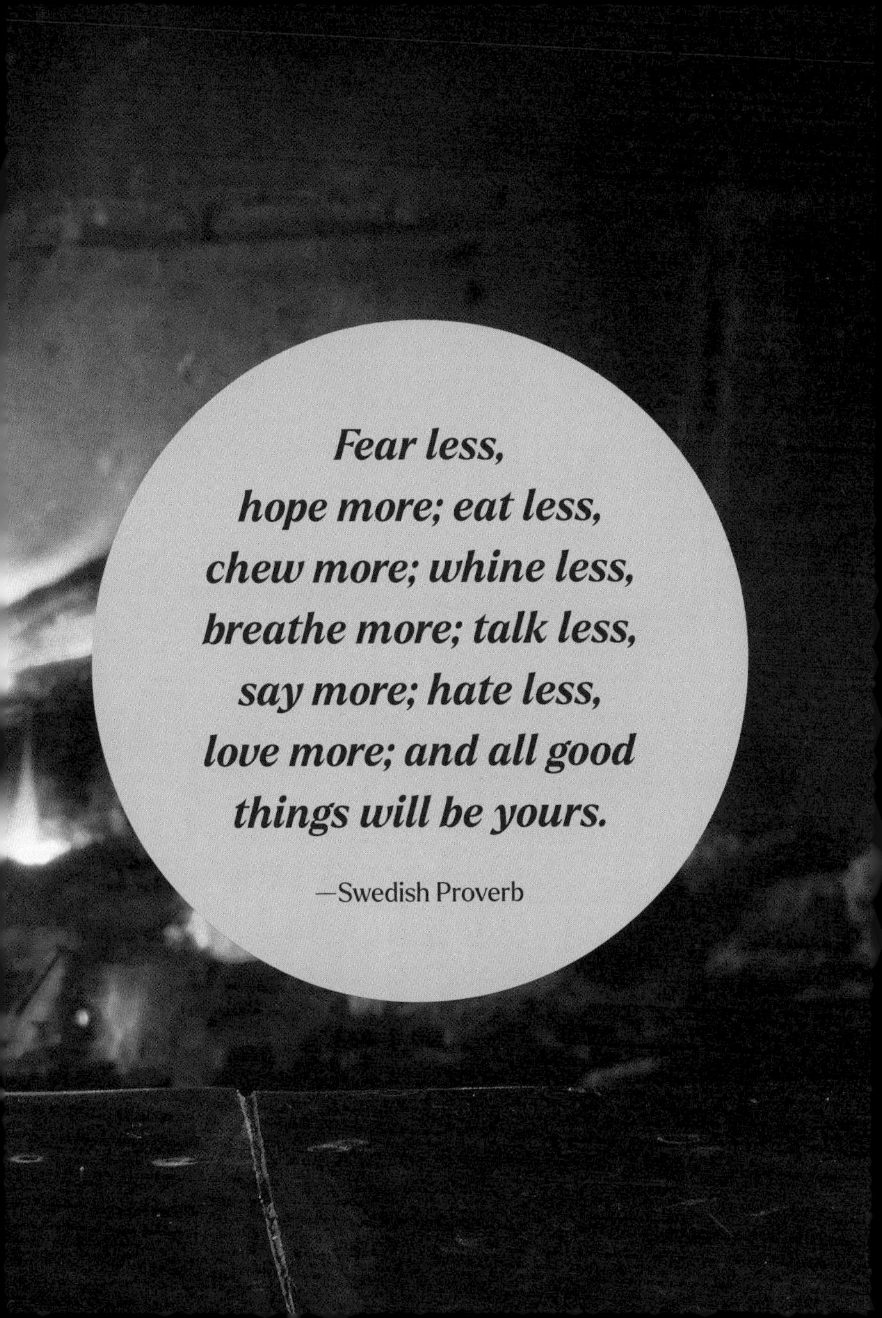

Fear less,
hope more; eat less,
chew more; whine less,
breathe more; talk less,
say more; hate less,
love more; and all good
things will be yours.

—Swedish Proverb

The Role of Aromatherapy

Breathing is cyclical, whether you are tentatively, softly sharing something you've been holding tight to your chest or inhaling in a sweet fragrance emanating from a flower blooming in your garden. Scent, more than any other sense, has the potent ability to unearth memories; think of the comforting scent of library books, or the way your stomach plummets any time you walk past someone who is wearing the same cologne as a former lover. Appreciation of different scents makes up a crucial part of my creative ritual – when I get to my writing desk, after I've used a tuning fork to clear my mind, I often light a candle or an incense burner to evoke a sense of indulgence, abundance and reward. It becomes my way of treating myself for committing to a period of creative productivity, rewarding myself like a little child. In the same way that my purchase of one of those fish-shaped jugs – that gurgle and make a bubbling sound when you pour out of them – helped me drink more water because I found it so entertaining, my dependence on various activities that awaken the sense of smell is a vital part of energizing me. My morning coffee, for example, is a key part of my routine but I've also begun to distil my own scent sprays at night to help me unwind in the same way.

Creating your own sprays and oils for aromatherapy

I love infusing my own scents, particularly using all the wonderful things my husband is growing in our garden. The trick is to pick your plants at dawn or dusk as this is when the scent is at its most potent, because as the sun gets higher in the sky the sunlight will make the scent diffuse into the atmosphere, which makes for a beautifully scented garden but a less powerful ingredient to work with.

Pick your plants and lay them out for a day or two on a paper towel, which will allow any creature taking residence in the plant to leave its confines with dignity – and sparing it from a fairly sticky fate! Then it's the fun part – infusing your own oils.

I love using a combination of plants like peppermint, lavender, rosemary, jasmine or rose to create a lightly scented oil to apply to my skin or at my temples. Plants like calendula (not *just* for tea!) have wonderful soothing and healing properties – the trick is of course to do your research and do spot tests on yourself first before applying something all over. For infusing an oil for use on the skin (which is lovely to put in the bath, too), I'd start with a sterilized clear jar, submerging the dried petals with a high-quality cold-pressed oil – something like argan, jojoba, grapeseed or extra virgin olive oil. Ensure the plant matter is submerged in the oil, and let the sunlight do the hard work of infusing the ingredients by keeping the jar near a window. Gently shake the jar every so often for a period of around six weeks. Once infused, strain using a mesh strainer or cheesecloth, before decanting into a dark container to ensure it keeps.

For sprays, I tend to fill three-quarters of whatever spray bottle I'm using with witch hazel and then top up the remaining quarter with distilled water before adding around thirty drops in various combinations of pure essential oils. I spray this across my pillow before I go to sleep – eucalyptus and lavender is a particular favourite of mine – but I'm partial to rosemary and rose as well.

Kōdō: The way of incense

Much of my childhood was spent in Japan with my maternal grandparents, from whom I learned a deep appreciation of a life imbued with creativity and spirituality. My Japanese grandfather, in

particular, was closely in touch with the ways in which the arts and other mindful practices could allow him to think creatively, and the balance he achieved, particularly when it came to his work life, was something I was inspired to write about in my early works. He was a businessman, a senior executive at an oil company but one who came from humble beginnings; however, the side of him I knew – the man he was at home – dedicated his time to things like painting, flower arranging, cooking, and gardening. He would spend his time at home with us in this way, enjoying his daily long baths, or telling us stories that he would illustrate before us using a set of watercolours. He spent a lot of time at the temple, too, and from there I learned more about the mindful effects of incense, particularly the *kōdō*, or the way of fragrance.

Similar to *ikebana* (the way of flowers) or *chado* (the way of tea), the way of incense is a classic art of refinement in Japanese culture, one with a long history and complex set of rules around it. There are ten virtues or benefits (known as *kōnojūtoku*) that underpin the artform:

1. It brings the other senses into sharper focus
2. It is able to purify not only the spirit, but also the mind
3. It has the power to reduce or eliminate polluting influences
4. It can energize and awaken the spirit
5. It has the power to bring people together, eliminating a sense of isolation or loneliness
6. It has a calming effect during times of uncertainty
7. It is not overpowering
8. It does not require too much
9. It has longevity
10. It does not cause harm

Traditionally, the practice involved lightly heating material like cedar wood, using instruments to gently impart the scent, rather than burn it outright, taking a subtle, muted approach. Yet there are playful elements to the art too – games like *genjiko*, which invite the participants to guess different scents, or compare similarities in order to pique and heighten their enjoyment.

Another key part of *kōdō* relates to the approach taken by the practitioners of not reducing the practice to smell alone. The idea is to properly appreciate the way of fragrance through a more holistic approach, one that engages sensations beyond smell alone, by *listening* to the material, the response made by your body, by observing the interplay between all the variables – seasonality, timing and setting.

The art of *kōdō* serves as a reminder, for me, that we are part of something greater, but is also a physical embodiment of the ideals we may be trying to emulate through our work. It is the mindful application and appreciation that has a transformative and almost magical power to it, one that I seek to include and incorporate into the way I see the world, and the way I want to create.

No man can taste
the fruits of autumn
while he is delighting
his scent with the
flowers of spring.

—Samuel Johnson

A TRADITION OF BOOK GIVING

One of my favourite things in the world is the smell of books. Old books in particular, but I'm partial to that boxfresh scent too – something you don't really get with an e-reader. Books are always my favourite thing to receive as a gift, and there is a winter tradition in Iceland that brings loved ones together through a shared love of literature – Jólabókaflóðið. Books are gifted and exchanged, making this solitary pastime more communal, a celebration of books where the evening might be spent devouring your new acquisition.

Putting It Out There: Finding Someone to Listen

With any creative endeavour, unless the merit comes from the process itself, the objective is for it to eventually be shared – to connect, resonate and evoke emotion in others. For a very long time, diary and letter writing was something I did purely for pleasure, but it was only when I published my ramblings on a blog that my work took on a life of its own. It resonated with others, which was a surprise to me, the person who had thought she was writing purely for the benefit of her grandmothers (the most engaged and receptive audience a girl could ask for).

Sharing creative work is like offering up a piece of your soul – egos can be fragile. Advice, unless specifically sought, can be incredibly off-putting and even borderline offensive – I'm sure any new parent can attest to that fact whenever a stranger berates their parenting style. Try not to be the boorish stranger, and raise the hackles up, but extend the *offer* of advice first. One of the ways in which I've managed to build a thicker skin and a sense of heightened resilience has been to do this in reverse – by trying to understand

unsolicited advice as coming from a place of infinite kindness, rather than hostile judgement. Nothing can shake a sensitive and creative being more than a rash negative outburst or an early bad review – but the wisdom and advice imparted from someone with whom you've been able to have a constructive dialogue, or whose opinion you admire that is given thoughtfully and considerately, only has the power to deepen your understanding and provide lasting benefit. This is another stage – to be willing to be adaptable and fluid, and not to be too precious during this period of exchanging ideas and opinions. Nothing is sacred. We are still advocating for play but we're shuffling the deck to deal out to others, rather than continuing to play solitaire.

The ability to share with others comes from being comfortable with vulnerability, from letting yourself be exposed to the elements, in the hope that you will be rewarded in turn with warmth and compassion.

The times where winter traditions are most commonly celebrated deal closely with themes of death and rebirth, feast and fallow. It follows that these times have a bittersweet quality and poignancy to them, and as we move through this cycle, we are presented with cues to demonstrate what we have learned. The ways we might need to adapt to remain and become resilient.

Purification Rituals: Burning Sage and Palo Santo

The symbolic purification of a space can be conducted through the burning of sage or palo santo wood. This ritual has roots in Egyptian, Roman, Greek and Native American cultures, and is sometimes practised as part of winter solstice rituals.

Lighting with intention, ethically sourced dried and tightly packed bundles of sage (Californian white sage) and palo santo wood are set alight for 20–30 seconds, before being blown out (by gently waving in the air). Moving around the space, which you will have prepared beforehand by opening any doors and windows to allow for adequate ventilation, you allow the smoke to dissipate and 'cleanse' the space, to be filled with positive energy and intentions. When burning sage, it's important to be respectful and mindful of the fact that it is a practice adapted from the sacred rite of 'smudging', which is ceremoniously practised by some Indigenous communities in the Americas.

Speaking with Intention

Around the different moon cycles, I like to speak to myself. I admit, it sounds alarmingly like witchcraft, or some kind of dark art, but it's the timing, more than anything, that works for me. I do it daily, monthly, quarterly, the intentions I set about what I'd like to do becoming bigger and greater the less frequent it is. For example, in the mornings I like to write about how I'd like to feel, or what I would like to do, and speak it out loud. 'I want to be happy today.' 'I am energized.' 'I'm going to feel inspired to write.' These ambitions become greater: 'I'll meet someone interesting, who sparks my creativity.' 'I will write another book.' Hearing myself say these things out loud is a way I hold myself accountable – even if it's only the dog that hears me. There's something comforting in hearing it in my own voice, making it easier to believe that I can do it. That I can make it happen. As if I'm tricking my*self* – when I remember myself saying I would do something, it makes me more likely to put it into action and actually *do the damn thing*.

Feelings are easier to speak about with intentionality, as are loose plans. 'I am going to buy a $5.2 million dollar house on Malibu beach', is just too specific a request to be feasible, in my opinion – but hey, maybe I'm just thinking small. But when doing this work, whether it is using tarot cards to do some soul-searching, or by trying to conjure up feelings aspirationally, it's more important to focus on the *why* – your feelings, emotions, state of being – rather than the *what* (material things).

I had a similar list for myself before I turned thirty. It contained things like 'I want to write a book' – the publisher's email came two months afterwards. I wanted to buy a house, which seemed impossible at twenty-three – and yet my job, combined with the opportunities that came along with my first book and a stable partner, helped me to do so. I didn't accomplish everything I had spoken about with intention, but having expressed these desires meant I began to work towards the things I wanted for myself – often in the most minute ways. In the same way that we work towards *listening* to others as part of our creative process, I find that *speaking* with thought and meaning has an almost mystical power to it. You see it in ancient forms and practices; yoga, for example, often starts with the practitioner invited to set their intention. It's not just about one day, but every day after that. Or for the next hour. Even the most mundane tasks can be imbued with meaning when approached with intention. This is no doubt further instilled in me due to my Japanese upbringing and the concept of *kotodama*, meaning the spirit or soul of words. It is the notion that language has power, a mystical power that can be evoked or conjured. And so I like to say these things aloud, not because I'm speaking to a higher power or the spirits of my ancestors, but to ask these things of myself. To spark hope and confidence in my own abilities, an oath or promise to dedicate myself to bringing to fruition the things I need to in order to get to the place I'd like to go.

Speaking with Gratitude

I have always regretted things I have left unsaid. As a child, I was painfully, excruciatingly shy, and while I seem to have matured out of that stage, I often decide to not tell people how much I admire them, in fear of embarrassing them or appearing too forward. A few hard lessons have softened this rigid habit of mine – witnessing first-hand the breakdown of parental relationships, time after time, but also the death of a friend by suicide – moments like these can feel life-altering and full of sorrow, but I find myself taking some of the blame. Not that I could have prevented these things necessarily, but I know that in the darkest moments being seen and understood or appreciated by another can be a momentary salve in an otherwise desperate situation.

I try to speak to others now with appreciation and gratitude. If I enjoy someone's work, or have been moved by it, I try to tell them the ways in which they've inspired me. If someone has reached out and provided comfort in moments of pain, I try to thank them. I have been blessed with the most patient friends and have been treated with kindness at the times I've been unwell and not equipped to treat myself in that way.

Nothing is lost when you are gracious, and when you speak with truth, honesty and a lack of agenda. Gratitude is about appreciation, without the assumption of anything in return – but it often comes back to you anyway. Thank those who have inspired you and have supported you and will continue to do so. Thank those who have had a fleeting but memorable and meaningful influence. Find the joys in the little things around you, and in return the majesty in the mundane will make itself known.

Chapter 5

How to Taste
Finding the time to savour

My husband, an anaesthetist, will often come home after a draining shift at the hospital to be greeted first by the enthusiastic barking of our 4.5kg and rather neurotic miniature dachshund Milhouse, followed by me – usually in some dishevelled state – wanting to know what he has eaten that day. If I've packed him a lunch, the questioning will often be about how he liked the food – if it travelled well, how he ate it, when he ate it, and so on. A similar and more persistent line of questioning will take place if he's had to find sustenance elsewhere. It's a habit passed down from my mother, and her mother before her. My grandmother's solution to mending my broken teenage heart was by taking me out for steak, followed by a chocolate parfait (which she ended up eating herself). It comes from a deeply held belief that food is sustenance – for the body *and* the soul. What is no doubt an irritating habit of mine, particularly to someone who has spent countless hours on his feet, is really about my desire to ease some of his burden – to help him be nourished and, in turn, show my affection.

In moments of sadness and despair, my appetite is often the first thing to go. The same can be said when I am trying to find a burst of inspiration or creativity – I decide to limit myself of distractions and try to focus elsewhere, all while forgetting that the best ideas come from the most unlikely sources.

To think creatively, we need to welcome creativity into our lives in all its forms – and that includes eating well.

As a food writer and restaurant reviewer, as well as having experience working in kitchens and in front-of-house positions, I've seen this first hand. From the chef who became increasingly creative with their 'staff food', to the one who spent their weekends trying to reset and cleanse their palate by trying new restaurants, ingredients

Sour, sweet, bitter, pungent, all must be tasted.

—Chinese Proverb

HOW TO TASTE

and recipes – what we eat nourishes more than our bodies. Done correctly, it can feed our imaginations and souls too.

I have always believed that everyone is capable of creativity; in many cases we've just been weaned off it far too early. Some of my favourite stories are about those who found the time to devote to their passions later on in life; the courage to start tango dancing only after the kids have flown the nest, or those who find recognition after thirty years of consistent work. Then there are those who have the courage and conviction to know that all good things come to those who wait. Having patience and grace takes a certain type of bravery that is the result of careful cultivation.

My grandfather's orchard bears the most wonderful fruit. Much of it is bottled and preserved, but many of the trees that are the most productive were planted years before they would begin to flourish – planted by him with the knowledge that he would not get to enjoy the efforts of his hard work.

That, more than anything, is the enduring nature of love. To create and share – with much toiling and some suffering – without the expectation of enjoyment or reward. It is a compassionate, noble act, and one that serves as a significant reminder that one small contribution can have a lasting and enduring impact: to nurture, nourish and provide sustenance.

Savour the Flavour – Both Bitter and Sweet

Take the time to enjoy the moment. Your idea, project or creation has come from inception to fruition, and in life we so rarely take the time to create an event or ritual to celebrate the moments – from the memorable to the mundane. While not every single occasion is

When the soul hungers, even bitter things taste sweet.

—Latin Proverb

worthy of a celebration, it *is* notable and maintaining a nuanced palate is incredibly important. Take note of your achievements along with the failures. Learn from them and take them forward with you, for better or worse, they are part of your repertoire now.

Your palate is something that needs to be trained, both physically and metaphorically. This requires it to be challenged, which in turn requires it to be introduced to new and exciting things. Nothing will dull a palate or your mind more drastically than monotony – the same recipes every day or being exposed to the same thing over and over. Variety, they say, is the spice of life – and we require a vast spectrum of flavours to ignite our senses.

Nourishment takes many forms – many of these forms being interconnected, the same way a nutrient-rich soil results in an abundant harvest. When I'm suffering a period of creative blockage, or struggling to find the ways to become unstuck, I often turn to cooking and tasting as a way of self-care, but also to nourish myself spiritually.

I do this in four ways – the fresh, the fermented, the foreign and the familiar. What I can't achieve through one, I find in another.

The Fresh

After a particularly balmy August and September, there's nothing more striking than suddenly seeing the vibrant dark greens and punchy orange hues of the autumnal squashes taking over your local farmers' market. I have a similar feeling in the early summer months, when cherry season is upon us: that sense of delighted surprise (it's crept upon us so quickly), but also the notion of ephemerality or fleeting joy that it can provide.

The benefit of eating local (and organic, if possible) produce when it is in season is that it requires you to do less messing about with it for it to taste absolutely delicious. These things are often difficult to unlearn, especially when you might have become accustomed to getting your hands on specific fruits and vegetables all year round. I find that cooking seasonally encourages me to remain innovative – some of my favourite dishes have ended up being created because all I had to work with was the random assortment thrust upon me during a visit to a local market, or through my local community-run vegetable subscription service. In this small, almost imperceptible way, we are forced out of our comfort zone; once we get used to this on a micro level, we can begin to take greater and larger risks elsewhere too – with much (delicious) reward.

Another way to simplify the ways in which we cook and consume is by approaching it intuitively, rather than in a prescriptive manner. By this I mean approaching your grocery shopping – for a dinner party, for example – by engaging all of your senses. The first key is to never shop when you are hungry, and always be open to the fresh produce that catches your eye or evokes a strong memory. My most recent experience was driven by a memory of a delicious okra curry my mother used to make me as a child – so when a bowl of okra caught my eye at the vegetable market, I decided to take the opportunity to recreate my own.

Good medicine often has a bitter taste.

—Japanese Proverb

TIPS FOR COOKING INTUITIVELY

❋ **'Shop' your pantry.** The spices, unusual pasta shapes and different types of chutneys languishing in the back of your cupboard all deserve their time in the sun. Using a note keeping app, I keep an inventory of the items in my fridge, freezer and food cupboard at any one time, allowing me to keep track of what I have at home to work with, and what fresh ingredients I can acquire when I'm out and about, using what I already have as a guide.

❋ **Know your aromatics.** The herbs, vegetables and spices that you cook in some kind of fat – whether that is butter, lard or oil – are the canvas from which you will create. The foundation of my marriage comes from, I believe, a base of butter, garlic and fresh parsley – and yet some of my dearest friends abhor the herb with a passionate vehemence. Grated ginger and lemongrass cooked in coconut oil, however, evoke memories of time with my family when they lived in Cambodia, and clams cooked in either base take on an entirely different experience despite having the same 'hero' ingredient. Exploring different types of aromatics might be a good place to start if you're feeling stuck – but knowing what your likes and dislikes are from this level will allow you to be guided by what's seasonal, or on offer.

* **Taste and adjust as you go.** Cooking is all about balance, and there is an almost musical fluidity to it. Baking, in contrast, is less forgiving as it is mostly about science and precision. Cooking flatters the artistic temperament because it allows you to be a bit more experimental. You just have to taste and adjust as you go – you don't want to spend hours slaving over a dish, only to find later that you mistakenly used sugar instead of salt an hour ago. When in doubt, I find a dash of umami from soy sauce vastly improves most things it goes into, while a squeeze of lemon and a sprinkle of chilli can liven up a flat-tasting dish. The key is to tweak and taste constantly in order to become an expert at rebalancing (or salvaging) your evening meal.

* **Invest in high-quality staples.** Back in the days before hotdesking and remote working, I would inadvertently seek out kindred spirits in my office by having in my desk drawer a few non-negotiable staples – a pepper mill, a bottle of high-quality olive oil, and some balsamic vinegar. The olive oil in particular had the potential to turn a limp and rather lifeless-looking salad into something magnificent; and once word got around, I'd often have colleagues swing by my desk at lunch time (over time, I would develop an extensive selection of hot sauces in my drawer, too). While there are some things you can scrimp on, you can't beat an olive oil that can be eaten on its own, with some freshly baked bread, while also providing a fragrant dressing.

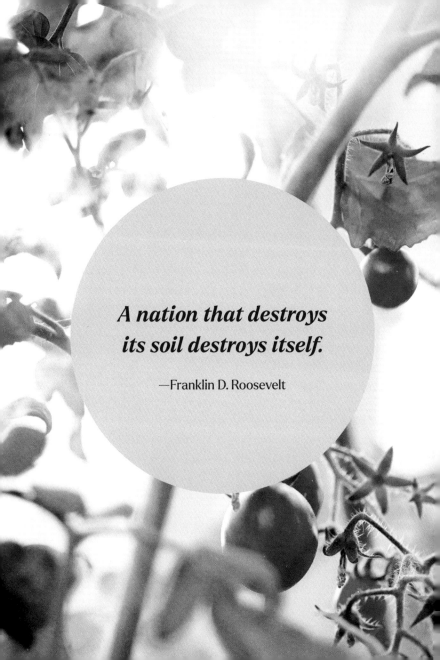

A nation that destroys its soil destroys itself.

—Franklin D. Roosevelt

NOURISHING YOU, NOURISHING THE PLANET

It all began when we bought a strawberry plant. We loved it, we cared for it and it was delicious. So we decided to get a tomato plant – another berry – just to keep it company. Nothing tastes as good as homegrown tomatoes. They taste like sunshine, and if anyone bottled the scent of the vines then I would wear it every single day like it was eau de parfum. To get the best tomatoes, though, you need to feed it; and before we knew it, we had begun to compost all of our vegetable peels and coffee grinds just to keep it happy.

I hated the process at the beginning – nothing could feel quite as foul as seeing worms feasting on the banana skins from yesterday's smoothie – and yet seeing the process at work, just how nutrient-rich the soil was becoming from it changed my outlook all together. My revulsion turned to wonder, then delight, then the most fragrant, colourful and sweet cherry tomatoes. They say one man's trash is another man's treasure, but when it comes to composting – it is the same man all along.

Maturation, ripening and decay are all part of life, and finding ways to repurpose this to bloom and grow further down the line is part of our role as the custodians of the earth.

The Fermented

I'm a big fan of pre-emptive cooking. At my most energetic, I might be found making batches of soup or broth ready to stash in my freezer for times when my energy levels are low, or if I'm ill, or to stave off a terrible mood. There is something different, though, about the process of fermentation – a happy gut can lead to a happy mind. The benefits of fermented foods that are rich in probiotics is something that I try to incorporate into my diet wherever possible.

This might have something to do with my early childhood in Seoul and Tokyo, for sure, but the act of preserving and fermenting is incredibly calming and meditative. My father would often prescribe kimchi for a variety of ailments, which as a teenager I found maddening, but now provides me with immense comfort; I love a warm bowl of *kimchi-jjigae* (kimchi and tofu stew) whenever I'm feeling a little weak and listless. My grandmother and grandfather would also spend the summer months boiling and bottling plums – the syrupy sweetness of the plums adding richness to a morning porridge year-round, instead of just during the summer days when the orchard is plentiful.

Whether you're fermenting or bottling, the first step is always the same – making sure you sterilize the bottles properly. You begin this process by washing your jars and their lids in warm, soapy water before placing them in a low oven (about 140°C) until they are completely dry (about 10 minutes).

The fermentation process also requires periods of rest – the slow, almost imperceptible changes to take place that can't be rushed. Like with the changing of the seasons, it requires nature to do the work; as a result, many different cultures have strong winter traditions with a ritual element when it comes to preparing ahead with food preparation, fermentation and bottling.

Sauerkraut

Take about 1kg of finely shredded cabbage and a tablespoon of salt. In a large bowl, combine the two and massage thoroughly, helping the salt draw the liquid out of the cabbage, which should take about 15 minutes. Drawing out the liquid is key, as this will be what the cabbage will be fermenting in for the next 4–5 weeks, preferably in a cool, dark yet well ventilated place. The liquid needs to cover the cabbage completely. Be sure to check in on the progress occasionally (through smell and taste).

Once the flavour is to your liking, then it can be served; if it isn't eaten all in one go (as often happens in our home), it should be stored in the fridge to maintain its optimal texture and flavour.

In Germany, sauerkraut and pork is a traditional dish eaten at New Year, symbolizing good luck and prosperity for the year ahead.

Kimchi

For the best results, prepare a 10 per cent salt brine (so 100g of coarse sea salt for each litre of water). Shred a Chinese or napa cabbage with some grated carrot, then immerse the cabbage and carrot in the brine and leave to soak for a couple of hours while you prepare the seasoning – a couple of chopped spring onions, 4 garlic cloves, 3 tablespoons of gochugaru (Korean chilli flakes), a teaspoon of sugar and some salt. For additional flavour, consider adding 2 tablespoons of shrimp paste or fish sauce, or its vegan equivalent (2 tablespoons of tamari and 2 tablespoons each of coconut sugar and lime juice). Drain the shredded cabbage and carrot, reserving some of the liquid, then combine the cabbage with the seasoning and pack it into a jar, topping up the jar with some of liquid from the brine to ensure that the ingredients are covered and submerged (this will prevent it from moulding). Leave to ferment in the same way as you would with sauerkraut.

Ways to enjoy kimchi include as a topping for noodles and rice-based dishes, incorporated into batter as part of fritters, or as a side with grilled vegetables and meat.

KIMJANG: THE FESTIVAL THAT CELEBRATES KIMCHI AS A COMMUNITY

Kimchi is a staple in Korean cuisine, and the preparation of it is part of Korea's intangible cultural heritage. *Kimjang* is the winter tradition of preparing and preserving the dish to last out the winter months and serves to bring communities and families together to do so. The tradition is a winter one that has pre-dated refrigeration, requiring a conscious awareness of the ways in which the natural world (the weather) might affect the fermentation process.

Kimchi-jjigae

One of my favourite winter meals, kimchi-jjigae (kimchi stew) feels like the epitome of winter comfort food. Spicy, sour and rich, the addition of kimchi provides nourishment and feels like it has healing properties. It's one of the things I crave the most when congested with a winter cold.

Depending on how the mood strikes me, I might prepare this with pork belly or mince, but for those who follow a plant-based diet, the dish can be made without it, too, provided you source a kimchi that is fermented without the use of animal products like anchovies.

1 tbsp sesame oil
1 small brown onion, finely chopped
1 garlic clove, grated or finely chopped
1 tbsp gochugaru (Korean chilli flakes)
1 tbsp gochujang (Korean chilli paste)
1 tbsp rice wine (mirin or similar –
    I use a dry sherry in a pinch)
1 tbsp soy sauce
150g pork belly or mince (optional)
150g kimchi (with the liquid)
100ml water or dashi stock
150g firm tofu
1 spring onion, chopped
Salt and pepper

HOW TO TASTE

1. Heat the sesame oil in a pan before adding the chopped onion and garlic, allowing them to soften so that the onion becomes translucent.

2. Add the chilli flakes, chilli paste, rice wine and soy sauce. Stir so that the aromatics are coated with the spice mixture. If you are using meat, then this would be the stage to add this in too, allowing the meat to brown all over.

3. Once the meat has browned slightly, add the kimchi along with all the water or stock and bring to the boil, then reduce the heat and simmer for about 15 minutes – you want the kimchi to be heated through and to release the flavour without compromising the texture of the kimchi.

4. Chop the tofu and stir it through, simmering for about 5 minutes before seasoning to taste with salt and pepper. Add the chopped spring onion for garnish and serve with rice or udon noodles.

Bottling fruit

To bottle fruit such as plums, as my grandparents used to do, the first thing you need is a sterilized sealable jar – the kind with a rubber seal made for preserving. Prepare the fruit: first by washing and then peeling. My grandmother always bottles her plums whole, which I love, but if you're not keen on leaving the stones in you can halve and remove the stones. For larger fruit such as apples, peaches and pears, I'd recommend peeling and bottling them in halves or quarters. Make a simple sugar syrup (3 parts water to 1 part sugar) by heating both together in a saucepan until the sugar has dissolved. Make sure your jar is warm before you add the syrup – you can do this by pouring in boiling water and then emptying it out. Add the fruit, then pour over the warm syrup and leave to cool slightly before closing the lid. Maintaining a strong seal is vital – which means you'll need to tap the side of the jars to ensure that there are no air bubbles trapped inside. I like to then seal the jars using a water bath method: place the filled and sealed jars in a large saucepan or stockpot, using something like a fitted rack inside the pan of water to ensure that the jars aren't in direct contact with the bottom of the pan (this reduces the risk of overheating). Pour enough water into the pan to ensure that the jars are completely submerged and bring to a rolling boil and 'process'. The processing time is the length of time you need to boil your jars and depends on the recipe but is usually 15–20 minutes for fruits like apples, plums and peaches and up to 35–40 minutes for tomatoes. After you've done this, place the 'processed' jars on your kitchen counter and leave to rest, undisturbed, for 12–24 hours; done successfully, this should create a seal that ensures that they are safe to be stored and eaten at a later date without refrigeration.

Bottled fruit can be used to make a trifle – with the addition of a sponge cake, custard and jelly – or made into a warming crumble, which just requires a low-effort combination of flour, butter and sugar to make the most comforting of winter desserts.

INFUSIONS

One of the ways you can stay resilient in the winter months is by capturing and enjoying ingredients and flavours of the summer, but in new and transformed ways. I love creating and infusing oils and vinegars with herbs and spices as a preservation method. Some herbs can be preserved from fresh – like basil, coriander or chives – by using a slow cooker method of heating the oil over a low, slow heat to capture the flavour. Fresh leafy herbs should be infused as soon as possible to get the best possible flavour from them; all they require is a little bit of heat to get that depth of flavour. Woody herbs, such as rosemary, sage, oregano and thyme can be hung upside down or somewhere cool and dark until they are ready to be infused. My favourite method is to place sprigs of the dried herb in a sterilized jar, cover with a good-quality extra virgin olive oil (making sure the herbs are fully submerged) and allow the sunlight to do its work. Leave for at least 6 weeks; the flavour will dissipate into the oil slowly and gently over time. After this period, it's worth transferring the oil into a darker container if you like a milder flavour or keep it as it is if you want your infusion to become ever more potent with time.

The Foreign

Be a culinary sponge. Whether it be through travel, a recipe in a beloved childhood book or an appealing package of some tinned sardines, surprise yourself by trying different local delicacies, new ingredients and unexpected dishes.

In my capacity as a food writer, but also having worked in the front and back of house at restaurants throughout my life, a common thread I found from chefs and creatives at the top of their game came from an almost constant need to be exploring and fine-tuning their palates. When I worked at an Italian small plates restaurant in Hackney, we would have monthly excursions to some other restaurants in our neighbourhood – pho at the local Vietnamese restaurant, injera bread from an Ethiopian place down the road, and so on. While it helped to see what we could learn from our competitors, it was more so that the staff could refine their palates, keeping the senses sharp.

As an inherently nosy person, my favourite way of doing this is to find out what others might be ordering. I'm lucky enough to speak to chefs in much of my work day-to-day, and through them I like to find out the things that they crave or what they eat in order to emulate their creative process – to find new perspectives, perhaps, in the dishes that others find comfort in, and find inspiration and to break a cycle of monotony that we can often find ourselves falling into.

Introducing more variation into our diet

A diverse and varied diet is key for health – by eating the same types of things day in and day out, we risk missing out on all the nutrients we may need. Eating seasonally is one way to make the habit stick, but also a much simpler way to ensure that you stick to the habit when you're short on time is to try eat at least five different colours a day,

particularly when it comes to your fruit and vegetables, as this can be a good way to make sure you are allowing the space for variation. Another way to take a proactive approach to planning your diet is to follow new guidance that suggests that eating thirty different types of plants a week will add more diversity to your gut microbiome. Meal planning is your friend here, something I do rigorously, not only to reduce food waste and make my household groceries go further, but also to find more energy – by ensuring I'm getting all the nutrients I need.

One way to break up the monotony of food that might not be working for us is to challenge ourselves to try new recipes – at least one a week. I made a new year's resolution to do this a few years ago; it's one of the ones I keep, year after year.

Eating together

One of the more significant changes my husband had to make when we began seeing each other was my insistence on eating most meals 'family style' – ordering a selection of dishes for the table to share through the use of small plates, rather than ordering dishes just for ourselves. His reluctance came from a fear of being short-changed, but the etiquette and the way to do this correctly is to have one person act as 'mother', serving and dishing out, rather than having it be a free-for-all.

Eating together and sharing is perhaps the most universal of winter traditions, and the act of sharing – of breaking bread together, nourishing each other – is one of the most wonderful parts of a big meal during this often bleak time.

The Swiss have a tradition of fondue and raclette, one that I have enjoyed as my father has lived there for several years. A similar communal sharing dish can be Japanese *nabemono* – hot pot dishes, and, of course, a show-stopping Sunday roast is a weekly ritual for many families.

The Familiar

My gluttonous nature is hereditary – inheriting the staunch belief that while food is medicine, it is also love, and work, and routine. My Japanese family in particular believe that you can measure the level of a person's emotional maturity by what cravings they have at certain points in their life – those who still crave the sweetness of a strawberry shortcake, for example, are used to being coddled and haven't yet had a taste of harsh reality. In contrast, someone craving the sharp, bitter flavours of smoked fish or the types of salted rice crackers that go well with beer, for example, might be going through a sullen or cynical phase. Sometimes we use food to describe how we would like things to be – after a heavy or stressful event you want the sanctuary of a molten bowl of mac and cheese, or the energizing refreshment of a breakfast smoothie.

Sometimes we just crave the familiar as we make our way on a journey – and that is a perfectly wonderful and natural thing. When the going gets tough, it is a soothing activity to recreate and evoke memories of times of safety. Food has the powerful ability to transport you there, and so we like to seek solace in this way. For me, this might be a big bowl of udon noodle soup to warm me up, or a chilled bowl of jelly to cool me down. Familiarity and comfort in taste can be the antidote to a particularly bitter period in your creative journey. Recreating this for others when they need it, I believe, can be one of the kindest things a person can do for another.

Mulling it over

In the winter months, the use of spices like cinnamon, cloves, star anise as well as citrus fruits can be a welcome balm and tonic. As well as the familiar mulled wine, cider and even ginger beer can benefit from this classic winter embellishment. Simply make a 'mulling syrup' that can be added to wine, cider or ginger beer at a later date – it is such a lovely winter gift (and one that can be enjoyed by those who might not want to drink alcohol). Depending on the quantity you'd like to make, add 4 parts water to 1 part brown sugar in a saucepan, along with one star anise, a cinnamon stick, 4 cloves and the peeled rind of an orange. Simply heat through slowly (don't bring it to the boil!) or use a gentle infusion method over the course of several months. Strain and store in a sterilized bottle. Alternatively, if using immediately, add the ingredients to a saucepan along with your 'mixer' of choice and taste as you go along. For one bottle of wine I like to add a star anise, a cinnamon stick, 4 cloves and 3–4 tablespoons of brown sugar to get the flavour (and visual effect) I like.

Food is sustenance – it is the way we are nourished, and the way we grow. It is necessary. Yet beyond being able to recognize and separate out the poisonous berries from the sweet, our sense of taste could be considered superfluous; instead the enjoyment we are able to get from taste and flavour is akin to a generous gift from some kind of benevolent higher power. We are learning while enjoying, through taste – finding enjoyment in simple pleasures, learning to trust our gut. We learn by doing and can take delight in the process while letting it nurture and nourish us, too. It can be bitter and unpleasant at times, but more often than not it is satisfying and enriching.

It is about letting the flavours sit on your tongue and savouring the moment. A meal can be prepared and shared with others, but the act of eating is personal. We all have different palates and tastes, all of which can evolve over time. What might have delighted a few years ago may feel saccharine and cloying at a later date – or have mellowed and matured.

As we take steps in our creative journey, we might consider the supporting role that taste can take as part of it. There are times that require us to be adventurous – to be brave and bold. To add heat and experiment with spice – to add an element of risk taking. Then there are the times we need to withdraw; to seek comfort and familiarity. To go back to our roots or explore our own legacies and histories. Both routes are valid and help to hone our taste. It might not be for everyone, but it has to sit right with you. It may require you to rebalance some elements – a little more salt here, a dollop of honey there – but like all the best dishes, it's best to go a more natural and authentic route, for the best type of nourishment.

Conclusion
How to grow

Love has its tides; before ebb tide you must take advantage of the flood.

—Chinese Proverb

We often think of winter as bleak. Inhospitable, desolate – devoid of life, warmth and hope. It tests your mettle. Survival is a test, not only the level of your preparedness, but the strength of your character. Only the most diligent woodland creatures who've toiled away all summer survive, but it's as much to do with luck as anything else. Sometimes life can feel like this – lacking in opportunity. Full of rejection, an unwelcoming environment.

In the process of writing this book, I had several personal setbacks of my own – a family breakdown on the eve of my wedding, a string of unexpected health problems, a period of financial uncertainty. It felt all-encompassing and – at times – like heartbreak. As if a period of hardship had no end. Again, this period forced me to find reflection and support within myself – to pause and use the time to find the strength to move forward and carry on.

The act of creating – the *doing* of it – is the magic in keeping your spirit alive. Just like the winter hives dialling down their industriousness, so do we in periods of *wintering* – focusing our energy in smaller, more acute ways, to avoid destruction altogether.

The ways in which we live are not conducive to periods of stillness, contentment and rest. I want to invite you to embrace, more often, life in the slow lane. Whether it's through stopping to feel the textures, inhaling the scent of a flower in bloom or waiting for your food to ferment, we desperately need to slow down, in order to go forward – armed with strength and power, after a period of rest and reflection.

*Nature does not hurry,
yet everything
is accomplished.*

—Lao Tzu

On Friendships

A strong familial connection is a wonderful thing, but we should never underestimate the significance of those we have chosen for ourselves. The caring, loving support of those who claim you without the ties of formal kinship can be the strength you draw upon in order to find true artistic expression.

It should not be taken for granted and is not an obligation that should be taken lightly. Our peers see us in ways our families often cannot, for who we really are. Maintaining these ties and connections is imperative to remaining balanced and objective. Our friends are our co-conspirators, our secret keepers and kind messengers. The company we keep are the best mirrors we have to the change we want to see in the world around us. Friendship requires investment and nurturing – an equal amount of give and take – but what we get in return is worth more than its weight in gold.

Be the friend you want by your side. Listen with compassion and act without fear, envy or jealousy. This is easier said than done and requires a great deal of generosity; to love selflessly and without fear. This is a challenge, but when you are overcome with negative emotions, attempt to stem the flow through communication, focusing on communicating the ways in which you are trying to understand your feelings, rather than focusing on their actions. Friendship is about sharing the load, and the best ones are with those who are also putting in the work to share the load, collaboratively offering to shoulder their portion of the burden.

On Discomfort

The nature of living is perhaps to be constantly seeking a level of relief from a sense of discomfort – the act of growing itself is full of messes, full of pain. It can be unpleasant to witness in ourselves – and perhaps more so in others.

Rejection can feel cruel and biting. This is part and parcel of putting yourself out there creatively, so to speak, and we need to find the ways in which we can soothe ourselves to weather it over time. This is the bee sting – excruciatingly painful in that moment, but one that numbs and wanes over time, until it becomes a mere memory.

Then there is a deeper type of pain, the kind that signals when something is truly wrong. This is a hollow pain, the type of all-encompassing abyss that feels capable of total and utter destruction.

Following the emotionally turbulent period that was the immediate aftermath of the pandemic, I became afflicted with a near constant level of physical pain. At its height, it impaired my ability to stand, to walk, to make any meaningful plans; the sense of sheer powerlessness left me bereft. This was nothing in comparison to the feeling of simply not being believed by medical professionals – dismissed, overlooked and ignored. The feeling of not being believed was arguably more painful than the feeling itself, or at least heightened the matter for me immensely. At times the only thing that kept me going was the belief that I had in myself that there was something greatly amiss – and only when I finally found a medical professional who took the pain seriously and worked with me to find an appropriate pain management plan, did I feel a sense of security to begin to create again.

I'm one of the lucky ones. Not everyone is quite as fortunate as I was in this regard. My only learning from that dark period of my life is to never stop believing that you are not aware of how you feel – *you*

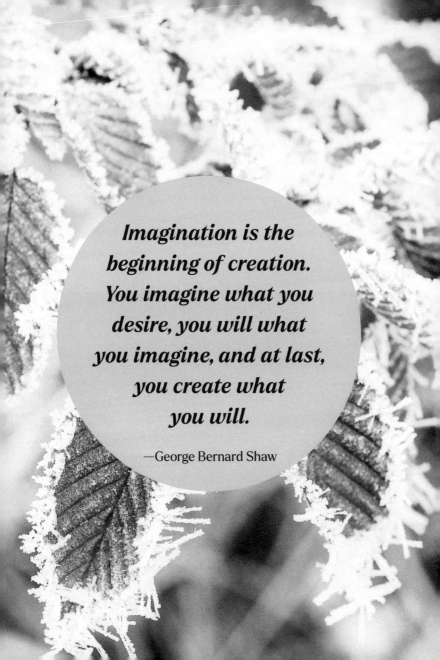

Imagination is the beginning of creation. You imagine what you desire, you will what you imagine, and at last, you create what you will.

—George Bernard Shaw

are the world's leading expert on yourself. Do not give up advocating for yourself. Whether it is through a period of physical or emotional pain, or trying to define where you stand on a certain issue or how you want to market yourself, remain in power. Own your authority. Be your own stalwart supporter. The physical and emotional pain from this period are ones that will stay with me for a long time. The thought is disarming and frightening. Like the Japanese art of *kintsugi* – repairing ceramic with golden lacquer – the wounds and scars make up part of an intricate pattern, a beautiful and delicate part of my identity. We can be broken and still shine – fractured but with the capacity to be repaired.

On Waiting

The fleeting life of the summer bee compared to the harsh and enduring winters faced by the winter ones so aptly captures the way it can feel when we are waiting for our own fruition – whether that is hearing back on a creative proposal, or plugging away at an endeavour that has yet to take off. At a certain point we must make peace with the state of waiting – find ways to become accustomed to a near constant state of limbo. It is frustratingly dull – the difference between a restful night of sleep and an evening spent twitching anxiously under your bedclothes.

Under the heavy winter snow, despite the bare-limbed trees, a near constant process of renewal and regeneration is occurring – both as a result of your efforts and independently from you altogether. Do what you can, and then wait – sending it off with a mixture of hope and with the best of good intentions.

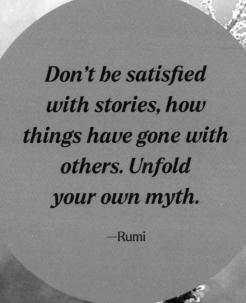

Don't be satisfied
with stories, how
things have gone with
others. Unfold
your own myth.

—Rumi

WINTER SOLSTICE TRADITIONS

A beautiful and ephemeral reminder of the passage of time, traditions that mark the winter solstice serve as a way to honour the season just past, closing the period with gratitude and reflection while welcoming in the season ahead.

Shab-e Yalda: In Iran, the winter solstice is marked with a feast to celebrate the coming lighter days and enjoy the longest night of the year. Summer fruits like pomegranates, watermelon and nuts are eaten to mark the occasion.

Toji: Yuzu, the winter citrus fruit, is a part of Japanese *Toji* (winter solstice) celebrations, where you might draw yourself up a bath infused with yuzu to cleanse and purify yourself.

Watching the sunrise: Stonehenge in England and Newgrange in Ireland are host to celebrations of the winter solstice, where revellers mark the occasion in the same way their pagan ancestors may have done years ago.

Vision without action is a daydream; action without vision is a nightmare.

—Japanese Proverb

On Renewal

The process repeats itself in an infinite loop, yet every year differs from the one before. In the same way, we have the potential to embrace the changes within ourselves and our identities. It is not natural for things to remain the same, the constant is change – and through renewal we have the potential to try new things, experiment with our identity, explore our own narratives.

As the moon waxes and wanes, so might our interests, passions and direction. The most challenging aspect of this comes when you attempt to create self-consciously. It can be hard to find your own North Star when you're worried about how you might appear to others. This exploration and maturity is a natural state of being – embrace the process wholeheartedly. Find play and improvisation with your sense of identity, while holding close your guiding values. Acknowledge the sacrifices and achievements you've made along the way of the journey, without letting it define or have the final word while you're still only part way.

The winter periods – the quieter, colder, perhaps more solitary moments – of our lives provide a much-needed respite for the industry of spring, the carnivals of summer. A time for introspection, dedication and focus, where – free of distraction – we can find clarity and focus to truly understand our values and find our voice in the comparative silence.

*Never doubt
that a small group of
thoughtful, committed
individuals can change the
world. In fact, it's the only
thing that ever has.*

—Margaret Mead

As much as we love the heat and sense of celebration, we are part of an intricate ecosystem – and like all the other creatures in the food chain, need to honour our biology and habits, too.

To do this, we must embrace the guiding power of our senses. Connect with our environment, find our centre of gravity. Contentment and satisfaction can come from a clear understanding of our place in the universe – and interpreting our own behaviours within the context of the natural ebb and flow of the world around us can have an enduring and calming effect.

In winter, we are slow. Slow to leave the comfort and warmth of our beds. Quick to find delight in nursing a hot drink with some dear friends near a warm fire. The rhythm and the pace of winter reflect the environmental pressures we go under. In the face of the season's brute force, we seek tenderness, rather than trying to compete in a losing battle. It is through this time – the slowness and stillness – that we draw upon our stores and resources, gather ourselves, to begin to plough on.

WHAT WE CAN LEARN FROM WINTERING FOR CREATIVE LIVING

1. Fallow periods are necessary – rest, recuperation and periods of silence are a necessary part of the creative process.
2. Trust in your senses to bring you back into balance.
3. Inspiration can come from anywhere.
4. Getting it down makes it tangible – it gives it potency.
5. Not all progress is visible. Some is beneath the surface – it doesn't have to be physically apparent to have meaning.

I sometimes find myself with Japanese words on the tip of my tongue, the result of being raised by a mother whose native tongue differs from the place I grew up in. One such word I find myself seeking on the cusp of winter is *kogarashi*, or 'leaf wilting wind'. The first sharp, cold bite in the air signalling the onset of winter. After a turbulent and intense period – whether that be personal or professional – I've begun to recognize the signs of that early winter warning in my soul, too.

Whether it is through meditation, or other methods of self-soothing, this time signals a need for peace, and to retreat. Finding joy in this quietly beautiful and majestic season, one stage at a time.

Creativity takes courage.

—Henri Matisse

Picture credits

p1 plainpicture/Stephen Shepherd; pp 2–3 Leonid Ikan/Getty Images; p11 Christopher Crawford/Alamy Stock Photo; p12–13 Songquan Deng/Alamy Stock Photo; p14 Goddard on the Go/Alamy Stock Photo; p16–17 Andrew Bret Wallis/Getty Images; p19 Eli Wilson/Getty Images; pp20–1, 120–1 DEEPOL by plainpicture; p22 plainpicture/Design Pics; p23 Olga Miltsova/Alamy Stock Photo; p24 Ulrick-T/Alamy Stock Photo; pp25, 32, 36, 156 plainpicture/KuS; pp26–7 Trudie Davidson/Getty Images; p28 plainpicture/Narratives/Jan Baldwin; p30 Blaza1980/Getty Images; pp34–5, 234–5, 249 plainpicture/HANDKE + NEU; p41 Claire Sheppard/Getty Images; p45 plainpicture/momento/Bronze Photography; p4 plainpicture/Ute Mans; pp48–9 John Finney photography/Getty Images; pp50–1 DEEPOL by plainpicture/Kateryna Soroka; p52 Elenathewise/Getty Images; pp55, 226–7 Jack Blueberry on Unsplash; p59 Annie Spratt on Unsplash; pp64–5 MarcNYC/Alamy Stock Photo; p66 Sergey Mironov/Getty Images; p73 Ja'Crispy/Getty Images; p77 Milamai/Getty Images; pp78–9 plainpicture/Marie Carr; pp82–3 Annemarie Gruden on Unsplash; pp84–5 Cavan Images/Getty Images; p87 Viva Luna Studios on Unsplash; pp92–3 Sean Gladwell/Getty Images; pp97, 216 10'000 hours/Getty Images; p101 plainpicture/Régine Heintz; pp104–5 Shangarey/Getty Images; p107 DEEPOL by plainpicture/Florian Löbermann;

p108 Artur Lynnyk/Alamy Stock Photo; p109 Imani Tulded on Unsplash; p111 DEEPOL by plainpicture/Aliyev Alexei Sergeevich; p113 rfranca/Getty Images; p115 William Leaman/Alamy Stock Photo; p117 NightandDay Images/Getty Images; p118 Roshan Bist/Getty Images; p122 plainpicture/Holly & John; p124–5 Pekic/Getty Images; p127 plainpicture/Aurelia Frey; p131 Patstock/Getty Images; p132–3 Maria Korneeva/Getty Images; pp136–7 Solovyova/Getty Images; pp138–9 Paolo Graziosi/Getty Images; p140 Anastasiia Shavshyna/Getty Images; p143 Michele Ursi/Getty Images; pp146–7 Geraint Rowland Photography/Getty Images; p151 DEEPOL by plainpicture/Dirk Wüstenhagen; p153 Ben White on Unsplash; p155 Halfpoint Images/Getty Images; p161 plainpicture/Ingrid Michel; p162 plainpicture/Spitta + Hellwig; pp166–7 DEEPOL by plainpicture/Manu Reyes; p168 Kevin McCarthy/Alamy Stock Photo; p169 Images Say More About Me Than Words/Getty Images; pp170, 213 DEEPOL by plainpicture/Zero Creatives; p179 Airam Dao on Unsplash; p191 Rob Wicks on Unsplash; p194 Adobe Stock; pp196, 204 Westend61/Getty Images; p200 Johner Imags/Alamy Stock Photo; p219 Kajetan Sumila on Unsplash; p225 Welat Odabasi/500px/Getty Images; p231 Feinschliff on Unsplash; p233 plainpicture/Baertels; p237 plainpicture/Design Pics/David and Micha Sheldon; pp238–9 Gary Mayes/Getty Images; p240 Alexander Trusler/Alamy Stock Photo; p241 Rodion Kutsaiev on Unsplash; p244 Artur Lynnyk/Alamy Stock Photo; p254 DEEPOL by plainpicture/Peter Rutherhagen. All other images, Shutterstock.com

References

1   www.ncbi.nlm.nih.gov/pmc/articles/PMC4419447

2   www.frontiersin.org/articles/10.3389/fpsyg.2014.00976/full

3   www.nature.com/articles/s41598-020-68632-9

4   https://pubmed.ncbi.nlm.nih.gov/32507429

5   www.standard.co.uk/news/health/cold-water-swimming-health-benefits-brain-study-b1058278.html

6   https://uvweather.net/blog/unlock-minds-potential-lower-temperatures

7   https://worldhappiness.report/ed/2018/

8   https://www.ncbi.nlm.nih.gov/pmc/articles/PMC6305886/

Acknowledgements

There are times within the process of creating that can feel incredibly lonely. There's the glory of having your name on the cover, but with it comes the trepidation and fear that you'll also be alone with egg on your face if things don't quite go to plan. A writer's ego is a fragile thing, and any new work requires self-exploration and a large amount of coaxing.

It also requires a great deal of trust. In your darkest moments, you might find yourself closing off, lest your ideas are shot down before they've had a chance to bloom. Deciding who to share things with and feeling like you're unable to turn to others during this process is the biggest challenge I find myself still working on.

Of course, this is hardly ever true, despite how overwhelming it can seem when you're still on this journey.

I'm inordinately grateful that I've managed to surround myself with so much kindness, empathy and support. I strive not to take this for granted, armed with the belief that this, as with all things, can change. I hope that I remember to tend to the things that are precious, spend time in ways to appreciate and cherish, and not to regret things left unsaid.

The ebb and flow of life is constant, and as the tide shifts, we often lose track of what we want to say. The wind snatches the words from our lips in the heat of a moment and often returns them back to us much later – sometimes too late. I know this, and yet I still find my effusive declarations of love and gratitude left unsaid out of fear, or not wanting to clear shards of eggshell out of my new fringe (clearly this egg-based-humiliation-phobia preys on my conscience more heavily than I have previously realized). I hope I move through this in person and begin to express myself with sincerity and delight and in ways that will leave no doubt in the minds of the recipients of my affection about how I feel.

For now, I want to acknowledge the people that make the day-to-day possible. I don't want to understate the importance of being adequately caffeinated as part of my writing process – and I'm deeply grateful for the cheerful welcome and excellently crafted cappuccinos from the team at Café Mélo. Georgia, Maddie, Paul and the team of dachshund assistants at Dachabout who take care of the most neurotic sausage dog in East London – thank you for the hours of silence crucial to the editing process, while providing updates that provide a sense of safety and a healthy dose of morale to keep me going. To Jenny Smith, whose lovely fortnightly presence always provides a sense of clarity as you help us sort through our chaos – 'Jenny Day' is always our favourite day of the week.

Then there are the people who are down in the trenches with me. To Matt Millett, Harriet Morris, Rachel Stephenson Sheff, Laura Percival, Nancy Hargreaves, Beatrice Liddell, Kimberley Peek, Cat Anderson – thank you for providing a helpful ear, comic relief and distractions both helpful and unhelpful.

To my in-laws – Paul and Alison Durrands, who are unwavering in their support, and generous beyond measure. Thank you for letting our dog terrorize the squirrels in your garden, disrupt your work calls and generally cause chaos during his frequent sojourns.

To the wonderful HarperCollins team, particularly Lydia Good, whose thoughtful insight and belief in this book and in my ability to create it is so important to me. Additional thank yous to Catherine Wood, Georgina Atsiaris and Clare Sayer for all of your hard work!

To my sister Amy, who has always been braver and wiser than me, despite being the younger one. I cannot begin to thank you

for your constant encouragement, support, kindness and the occasional reality check. I love you.

Thanks as always to the inspiring women that I feel privileged to have been supported and raised by. My mother Eriko and grandmothers Gilly and Motoko. My aunts – Jo, Lucy, Hilary, Junko and Taeko – and my 'stepladder', Katie. To my little siblings, Rosie and Clement – thank you for making me laugh, for keeping me proud of you always. To my father Bill, who continues to teach me every day.

I can appreciate just how ridiculous it is to address an acknowledgement to a creature that isn't literate, but I'm going to write one all the same. A sweet, fiercely loyal, loving little thing that doesn't even weigh 5kg soaking wet – thank you for your sense of humour, your protective spirit and ceaseless affection. Who's a good boy, Milhouse? You're a *good boy*.

And to my husband, Tom. Your enthusiasm, passion, work ethic and kindness never fail to amaze me. You are seemingly blessed with a generous capacity of spirit and feeling (and not to mention appetite). Thank you for picking me up, for problem solving and for being on this journey with me – one where we see each other, hear each other, hold each other – as we navigate and meet the joys and sorrows of life together.

ERIN NIIMI LONGHURST is a British/Japanese author living in London. Her work has been featured in *The Guardian*, *Time Out*, the BBC, *Vogue*, *Stylist*, *El Mundo*, *Elle Vietnam*, *Reader's Digest*, and MarthaStewart.com among others.

She is the author of *Japonisme* (HarperCollins, 2018) and *Omoiyari* (HarperCollins, 2020).

Her work is influenced by her dual heritage and focuses on her passion for food (having completed the Leiths School of Food and Wine Essentials Course), ikigai (finding purpose), ikebana (flower arranging), and shinrinyoku (forest bathing). She is incredibly passionate about holistic wellbeing and writes extensively about lifestyle and culture inspired by her multicultural upbringing (in addition to London and Tokyo, she has also lived in New York, Seoul, Belgrade, and Manchester). She is a member of the Guild of Food Writers.

She is currently in East London, where she lives with her husband and their sausage dog Milhouse.